ISLAM

FOR BEGINNERS™

N. I. Matar

Illustrated by

H. N. Haddad

Orient BlackSwan

ORIENT BLACKSWAN PRIVATE LIMITED

Registered Office
3-6-752, Himyatnagar
Hyderabad 500 029 (A.P), India
Email: centraloffice@orientblackswan.com

Other Offices
Bangalore / Bhopal / Bhubaneshwar / Chennai / Ernakulam / Guwahati
Hyderabad / Jaipur / Kolkata / Lucknow / Mumbai / New Delhi / Patna

Page Design and Typesetting: H.N. And S.C. Haddad
Cover Design: Suzetta Bozzi

Published by arrangement with
Writers and Readers Limited
P O Box 29522
London N1 8 FB

First Published by Orient Longman Private Limited 2002
Reprint 2004
First Orient Blackswan Impression 2008

ISBN 13: 978-81-250-2233 6
ISBN 10: 81-250-2233-3

Printed In India at
Novena Offset
Chennai 600 005

Published by
Orient Blackswan Private Limited
160, Annasalai, Chennai 600 002
Email: chennai@orientblackswan.com

بسم الله الرحمن الرحيم

To the Reader

◆ The meanings of the **Holy Koran** that will appear in the text are taken from the translations by Ahmad Ali, Arthur J. Arberry, A. J. Dawood, and Marmaduke Pickthall. The quotations from *Hadith* are taken from a translation of specific selections from Muslim and Bukhari.

◆ Whenever the name of the **Prophet Mohammad** appears, it shall be followed by ◗ to represent the Arabic words, "May the blessings and peace of God be upon Him" which always come after the Prophet's ◗ name.

◆ For facility, all dates in this text will refer to the Common Era (C.E.). To convert to the Muslim Hijra calendar, see page 28 below.

◆ Islamic tradition condemned the pictorial depiction of the Prophet ◗ and of the family of the Prophet ◗ in all artistic expressions. It further discouraged the representation of living creatures for fear that such representation would lead to pagan or polytheistic worship. As a result, Muslim artists did not imitate the external world, but conveyed its inherent meaning through the arabesque and geometric patterns. Whenever they chose to draw living creatures, they produced flat, two-dimensional illustrations that were deliberately unrealistic, with no illusion of depth.

◆ This book uses the multiple media of narrative, line drawing, calligraphy, and photograph. In all the line drawings, the illustrator has abided by the above criteria of Islamic art.

Table of Contents

The names of God and Mohammad ◗ in Arabic.

To Ibrahim, Hady and Seri.

REVELATION

Al-Fatiha

(The Opening)

"In the name of God, the Merciful, the Compassionate.

Praise belongs to God, the Lord of all Being,
the All-merciful, the All-compassionate,
the Master of the Day of Doom.

Thee only we serve; to Thee alone we pray for succor.
Guide us in the straight path,
the path of those whom Thou hast blessed,
not of those against whom Thou art wrathful,
nor of those who are astray."

Koran 1: 1-7

The above verses constitute the first chapter of the Koran and are the most widely invoked words in the world of Islam.

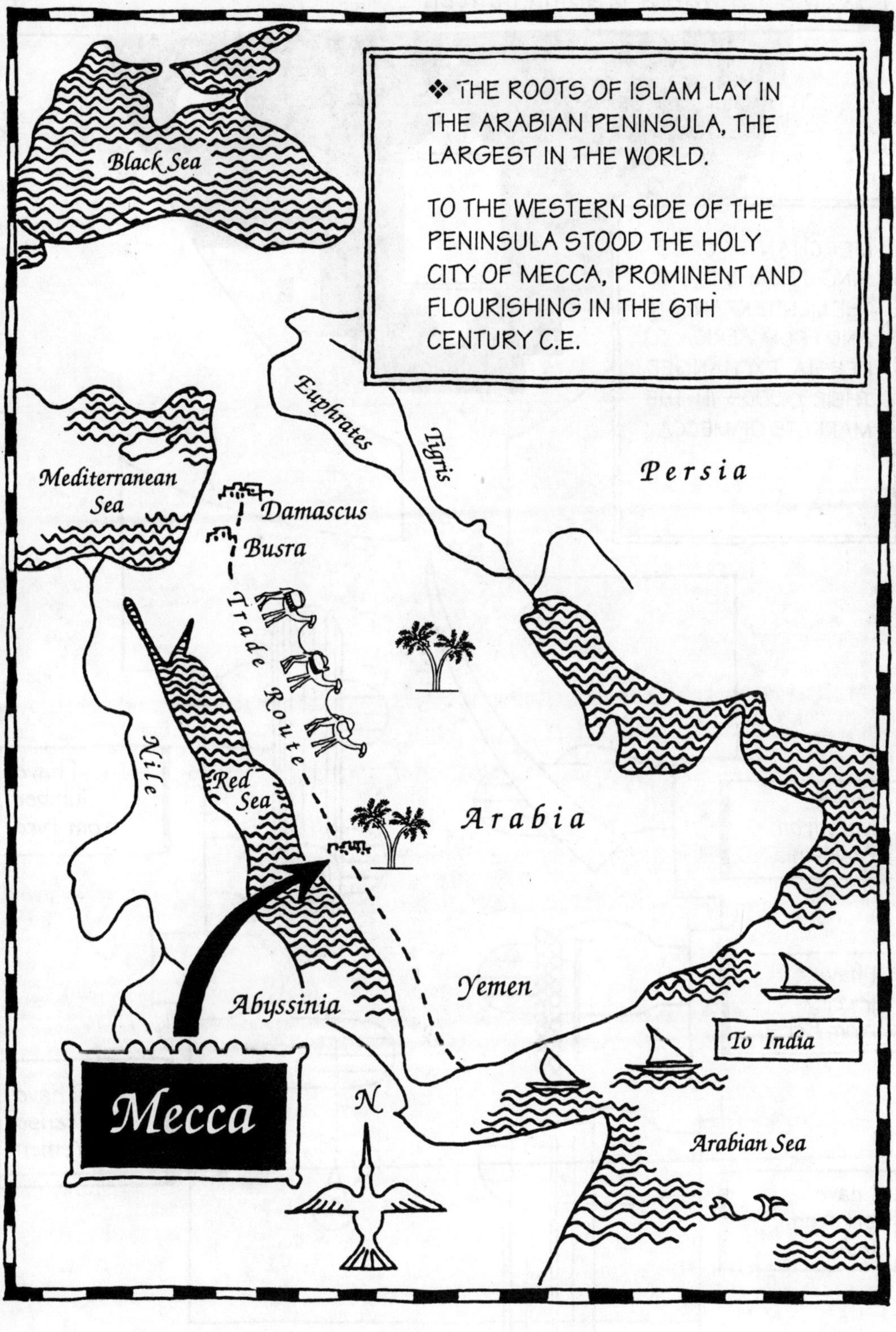
❖ THE ROOTS OF ISLAM LAY IN THE ARABIAN PENINSULA, THE LARGEST IN THE WORLD.
TO THE WESTERN SIDE OF THE PENINSULA STOOD THE HOLY CITY OF MECCA, PROMINENT AND FLOURISHING IN THE 6TH CENTURY C.E.
Black Sea
Mediterranean Sea
Euphrates
Tigris
Persia
Damascus
Busra
Trade Route
Nile
Red Sea
Arabia
Yemen
Abyssinia
Mecca
N
To India
Arabian Sea

1 Mecca was a trading center.

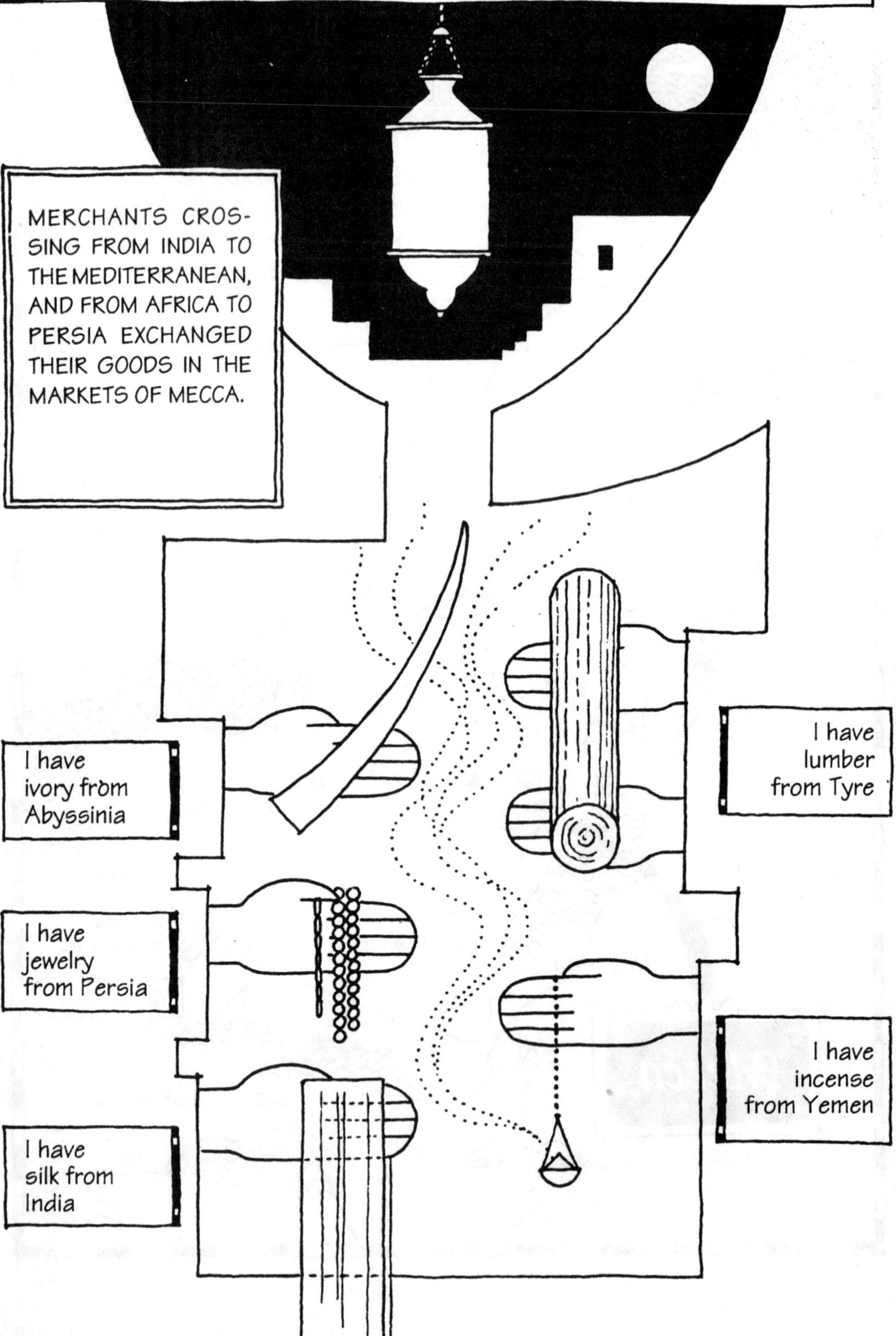

2
It was also a cultural center.
THE ARAB PEOPLE HAD A PASSION FOR POETRY.
Antara Bin Shaddad
LOVE POET
Nabigha Al-Dhubyani
ROYAL POET
Tarafa
SATIRIST
Imru'u 'l Qays
LEADING POET
Once a year, nomad poets gathered in the market town of 'Ukaz, east of the city, to recite their verse.

3 Most importantly, it was a religious center.

The Ka'aba was a house of Gods.

Once a year, Arab tribes went there on pilgrimage.

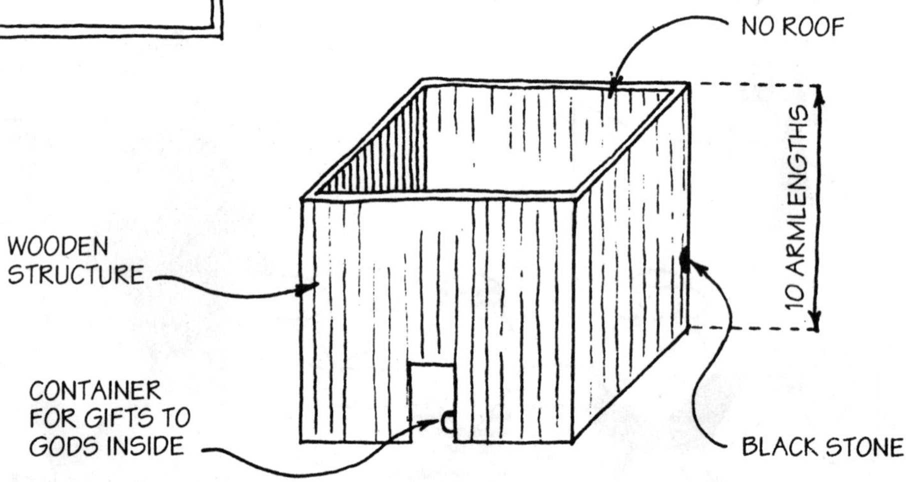

In Mecca stood the Ka'aba, a wooden structure encasing a circular black stone. Inside and around it were 360 deities brought by pilgrims from across the peninsula.

Those deities originated in Graeco-Roman mythology and most of them were female.

Manat was one of the oldest goddesses and was believed to control human fortune.

Al-Lat was the sun deity and was widely popular. Her name meant "The Goddess".

The Goddess Al-Lat

The Lion of Al-Lat

Al-Uzza, the "Mighty One", was favored by the Meccans, along with the Goddess Hubal, the tutelary goddess of the Ka'aba. The worship of these deities involved animal sacrifice.

There were, however, followers of monotheism in Mecca, as in the rest of Arabia.

❖

There were *Jews* who were well-established in Yathrib, a rival city to Mecca. Their chief tribes lived both within the city and in Khaybar, north of it. The Jews were part of the custom, language and nomenclature of Arabia.

❖

So were the *Christians* who inhabited Damascus and Hira in the north of the peninsula, Najran in the south and to a lesser extent, the Hijaz area. Christians were either Monophysites (Christ has one divine nature) or Nestorians (Christ is man born God). Both groups were persecuted by the Byzantine church and in the next century supported Islam because it offered them toleration.

❖

There were also *al-Hanafiyyeen*, followers of the monotheism of the patriarch Abraham (Ibrahim). Ibrahim al-Khaleel, "the friend of God", professed faith in one universal God and in celebration, built, with his son Ismail, the Ka'aba, the Holy Sanctuary. But after his death, polytheists turned it into a place of idols.

Kuraish was one of the Meccan tribes profiting from the pilgrims to the Ka'aba. The Kuraishites were dominant in Mecca's plutocracy and were unrivalled merchants in Western Arabia.

In 570 C.E., Abraha al-Ashram, the King of Yemen, attacked Mecca because the city was competing for trade with his capital Sana'a. He used an elephant transported from Abyssinia which frightened the Meccans who had never seen such an animal in warfare.

But God struck the invaders with "flocks of birds" and destroyed them.
That year was named by the Meccans "YEAR OF THE ELEPHANT".

In August of that year, a boy was born in Mecca and given the name Mohammad ◗ (praiser), an uncommon name at the time. His father, Abdallah, a Kuraishite of the clan of Hashem, had recently died. The child's mother was called Amina and she too died a few years later.

Little is known about Mohammad ◗ in his early manhood except that he participated in Meccan politics and helped in the rebuilding of the Ka'aba after it was destroyed by a flood. At the age of 25, he married Khadija, a rich Kuraishite widow, and prospered as a trader between Damascus, Busra, Mecca and Yemen.

Throughout his life, Mohammad ◗ had the title of Abul Qassim, "Father of Qassim", his first son.

Before his fortieth year, Mohammad ◗ had often seclude
himself in meditation. In Ramadan (July) 610 C.E., as he sa
in a cave in Mount Hira', two miles north of Mecca, Allah (th
name of God in Arabic) revealed His words to Mohammad
through the Angel Gabriel.

> That night of revelation is known as **"the Night of Glory".**

These are the first words that were revealed to him. Mohammad was an unlettered Prophet ◗, and what he recited were the wondrous verses of God (ayat ul-Lah), not man-made words.

(٩٦) سُورَةُ العَلَقِ مَكِّيَّة
وَآيَاتُهَا تِسْعَ عَشْرَةَ

بِسْمِ ٱللَّهِ ٱلرَّحْمَٰنِ ٱلرَّحِيمِ

ٱقْرَأْ بِٱسْمِ رَبِّكَ ٱلَّذِى خَلَقَ (١) خَلَقَ ٱلْإِنسَٰنَ مِنْ
عَلَقٍ (٢) ٱقْرَأْ وَرَبُّكَ ٱلْأَكْرَمُ (٣) ٱلَّذِى عَلَّمَ بِٱلْقَلَمِ (٤)
عَلَّمَ ٱلْإِنسَٰنَ مَا لَمْ يَعْلَمْ (٥) كَلَّآ إِنَّ ٱلْإِنسَٰنَ لَيَطْغَىٰٓ (٦)
أَن رَّءَاهُ ٱسْتَغْنَىٰٓ (٧) إِنَّ إِلَىٰ رَبِّكَ ٱلرُّجْعَىٰٓ (٨) أَرَءَيْتَ
ٱلَّذِى يَنْهَىٰ (٩) عَبْدًا إِذَا صَلَّىٰٓ (١٠) أَرَءَيْتَ إِن كَانَ
عَلَى ٱلْهُدَىٰٓ (١١) أَوْ أَمَرَ بِٱلتَّقْوَىٰٓ (١٢) أَرَءَيْتَ إِن كَذَّبَ
وَتَوَلَّىٰٓ (١٣) أَلَمْ يَعْلَم بِأَنَّ ٱللَّهَ يَرَىٰ (١٤) كَلَّا لَئِن لَّمْ يَنتَهِ
لَنَسْفَعًا بِٱلنَّاصِيَةِ (١٥) نَاصِيَةٍ كَٰذِبَةٍ خَاطِئَةٍ (١٦) فَلْيَدْعُ
نَادِيَهُۥ (١٧) سَنَدْعُ ٱلزَّبَانِيَةَ (١٨) كَلَّا لَا تُطِعْهُ وَٱسْجُدْ
وَٱقْتَرِب (١٩) ۩

"In the name of God, the Compassionate, the Merciful,
Recite in the name of your Lord who created
Created man from clots of blood.
Recite! Your Lord is the Most Bountiful One,
Who by the pen taught man what he did not know."

Koran 96:1-5

لا إله إلا الله محمد رسول الله

The revelation of the Koran (recited text) had begun, and would continue until the death of the Prophet ◗.

ISLAM
(submission to God),
the last revelation in monotheism,
was born.

How do I become a Muslim?

You should witness to the following:

"There is no deity but God, and Mohammad ◗ is His Prophet."

The Koran has one overpowering theme:

GOD has no associate, no rival, no like. In HIM is the beginning of the creation, and its end; to HIM the human soul should turn; by HIM the universe continues until the "Last Scream" of Judgement Day.

GOD is above human reasoning and imagination, whatever mankind thinks about HIM,

HE
is
ALLAH-U AKBAR

beyond and greater, transcendent yet imminent, infinite yet as close to man as his "Jugular vein".

In the Koran, God speaks in HIS own voice and words to humanity: HE reminds and threatens, guides and corrects, forgives and punishes. Most emphatically,

HE
is
"the compassionate, the merciful"
(Rahman) (Raheem)

بسم الله الرحمن الرحيم

Every Surah (chapter) in the Koran opens with these words:
"In the Name of God the Compassionate, the Merciful."
These words, known as the Bismillah, remind mankind that

GOD IS MERCY.

This message of Islam was accepted at first by only a handful of Meccans:

- the Prophet's ◗ wife,
- the Prophet's ◗ friend Abu Bakr known as The Believer ,
- and the Prophet's ◗ cousin, Ali bin Abi Talib

But within a few years, the faithful became noticeable by their prayers and rejection of idols. The Kuraishites feared that the monotheistic revelation would undermine the lucrative pilgrimage trade, and they began a wave of persecution. As a result, some of the Muslims fled to Ethiopia where they met the Christian Negus (ruler).

WHAT IS
ISLAM ?
~ NEGUS ~

BELIEF IN GOD,
IN JUDGEMENT DAY,
IN A UNIVERSAL MESSAGE
REVEALED TO PROPHETS
FROM ADAM,
ABRAHAM
AND JESUS
TO
MOHAMMAD,
WHO IS
THE LAST MESSENGER
AND
"SEAL OF THE PROPHETS"
(KORAN 33:40)

DID YOU SAY JESUS ?
YES, HE WAS BORN OF THE VIRGIN MARY,
IS THE PUREST OF PROPHETS
AND WILL RETURN AT THE END OF TIME...

These are the words which had been revealed to the Prophet Mohammad ◗ about Jesus and which the emigrants repeated:

"Whereupon he (Jesus) spoke and said:
'I am the servant of God. He has given me the Book and ordained me a prophet. His blessing is upon me wherever I go, and He has commanded me to be steadfast in prayer and to give alms to the poor as long as I shall live. He has exhorted me to honor my mother and has purged me of vanity and wickedness. I was blessed on the day I was born, and blessed I shall be on the day of my death; and may peace be upon me on the day when I shall be raised to life.'
Such was Jesus, the son of Mary."

Koran 19:30-34

◆ ◆ ◆

The Koran views Jesus as a Prophet born of God's Spirit but without any divine characteristics. Thus he was not crucified, but only appeared to have been. (Koran 4:155-169)

The Koran honors the Virgin Mary as a model of chastity. There is a chapter in the Koran named after her (*Surah* 19), and many verses praise the purity and devotion of her life.

"And of Mary, daughter of Imran who guarded her chastity, so that We breathed into her a life from Us, and she believed the words of her Lord and His Books, and was among the obedient."

Koran 66:12

IN 621 C.E., THE PROPHET ◗ UNDERWENT THE NIGHT JOURNEY, AL ISRA', FROM MECCA TO THE RUINS OF THE TEMPLE IN JERUSALEM. THERE, HE PRAYED AT THE "FARTHEST MOSQUE" (KORAN 17:1), SO-NAMED BECAUSE IT WAS THE PLACE OF WORSHIP FARTHEST WEST KNOWN TO THE ARABS.

In Jerusalem, and on a rock now inside al-Haram a-Shareef (Dome of the Rock), Mohammad prayed and was lifted to the seven heavens where he received a vision of the Prophets of monotheism: Adam, Jesus (Isa) and John the Baptist (Yahya), Joseph (Yusuf), Enoch (Idris), Aaron (Haroon), Moses (Moosa) and Abraham.

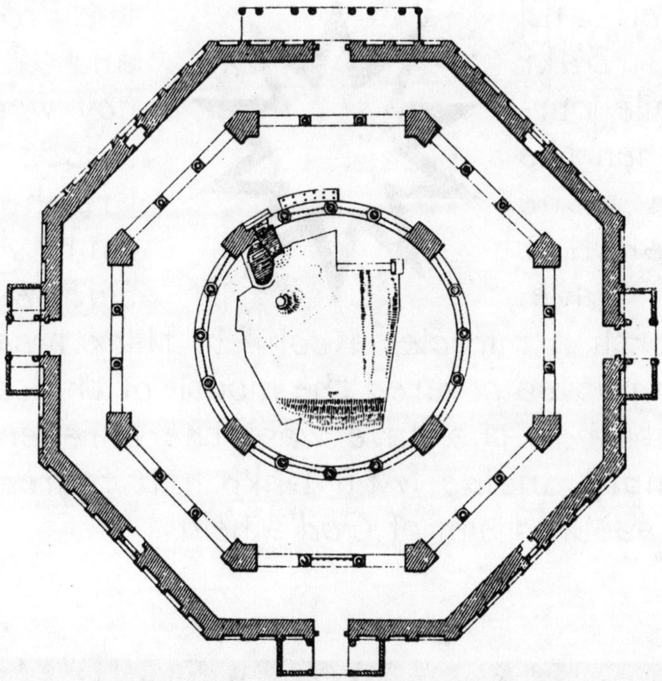

Plan of the Dome of the Rock, Jerusalem.

Whether mystical or physical (on the horse "Boraq", as the Prophet himself recounted), the experience of **al-Mi'raj** remains a mystery of God. Because of it,

Jerusalem is the third holiest city in Islam.

As Meccan hostility continued, the Prophet ◗ decided t leave his birth place for Yathrib where the Koranic teach ings had been well received. On the night of his flight, h learnt of a plot by the Meccans to kill him: he asked h cousin Ali to sleep in his bed so he could slip away. A cooperated and the Prophet ◗ le with Abu Bakr and a guide o the 275-mile jour- ney westward t Yathrib. When the Meccans caugh up with the Prophet ◗, h sought shelter with Abu Bak inside a cave. Suddenly, Go brought forth a miracle: a cobweb, thick tree branche and nesting doves covered the mouth of the cave. Seein how undisturbed the cave was, the pursuers though it was empty. Inside, Abu Bakr had feared, but th Prophet ◗ assured him of God's help.

> *"In the cave he said to his companion:*
> *'Do not despair, God is with us.'*
> *God caused His tranquillity to descend upon him and sent to his aid invisible warriors, so that he routed the unbelievers and exalted the Word of God. God is mighty and wise."*
>
> *Koran 9:40*

This emigration/flight took place in the summer of 622 C.E. It is the
HIJRA
whence the Muslim calendar begins.

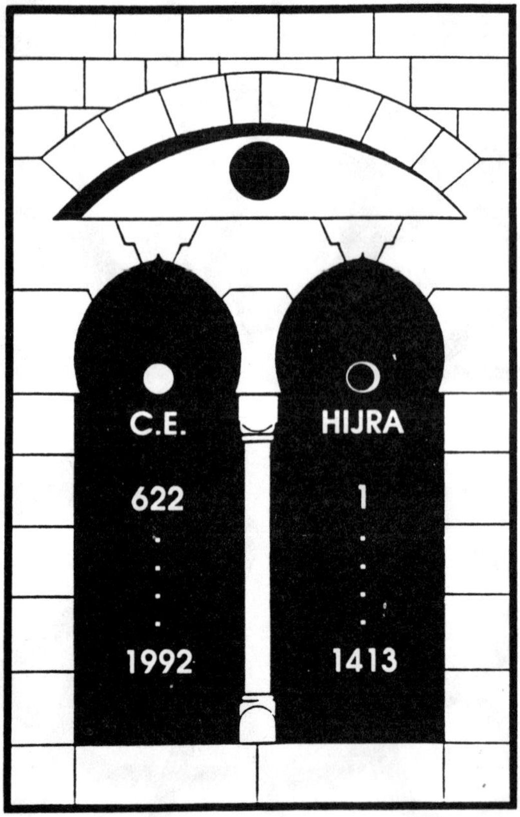

These are the months of the Muslim year:
Muharram, Safar, Rabee' Awal, Rabee' Thani, Jamadi Awal, Jamadi Thani, Rajab, Sha'aban, Ramadan, Shawwal, Dhul Qi'da and Dhul Hijra.

Because the year was measured by the lunar cycle, the crescent became the symbol of Islam. The lunar year is shorter than its solar counterpart by about 11 days.

To convert from Common Era to Hijra,
(C.E. - 622) x 33/32 = H

In Yathrib, the Prophet ◗ was welcomed by two groups of believers: the earlier emigrants from Mecca and the local supporters.

Henceforth, Yathrib became known as medinat al-Nabiyy, "City of the Prophet", MEDINA.
It is the second holiest city for Muslims after Mecca.

◆

In Medina, the Koran revealed the
SHARI'A
the Holy Law of the Islamic Theocracy.

❖ UMMA ❖
❖ JUSTICE ❖
❖ MANUMISSION ❖
❖ RIGHT TO LIFE ❖
❖ MARRIAGE ❖
❖ ADHAN ❖
❖ QIBLA ❖
❖ TOLERATION ❖

The religious, social and legal teachings of Shari'a, in their essentials, have guided Muslims into present times.

❖ UMMA ❖

The Arabs were a tribal people whose group bond was kinship. After the believers were separated from their relatives in Mecca, a new principle of cohesion was needed. God revealed the principle of **Umma** where the group bond does not depend on blood but on **faith in Him.**

Such a bond was evident around the Prophet ◗ himself: there was the Meccan and the Yathribite, the Persian and the African, the converted Christian and the converted Jew, the freed slave and the noble clan leader. All constituted the umma because they worshipped **Allah.**

❖ JUSTICE ❖

Before Islam, the blood-feud prevailed: when a member of a group was injured or killed by a person from another group, the first group had the right of vengeance, a tooth for a tooth, a life for a life.

The Koran praised the Muslim who accepted a penalty on the criminal which was less than the act penalized, or who forgave altogether (Koran 5:45, 16:126-127). Futhermore, the Koran distinguished in a novel way between deliberate and involuntary killing: if a believer deliberately killed another, he would be punished in hell: if accidentally, he would pay blood money.

Justice was paramount, not vengeance.

❖ MANUMISSION ❖

The Koranic principle of the brotherhood of believers was instrumental in extending compassion to all weak and dependent persons, particularly to the slaves. The Koran mitigated slavery by urging the Muslims to free the slave once the latter accepted Islam:

"Serve God and associate none with Him. Show kindness to parents and kindred, to orphans and to the destitute, to near and distant neighbours, to those that keep company with you, to the traveller in need, and to the slaves you own. God does not love arrogant and boastful men, who are themselves niggardly and enjoin others to be niggardly; who conceal the riches which God of His bounty has bestowed upon them."

Koran 4:36

Faith was liberation...

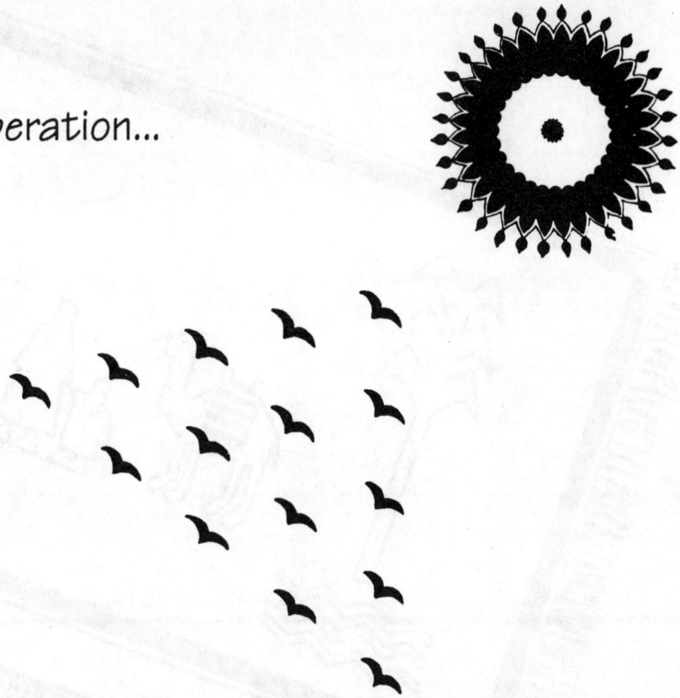

❖ RIGHT TO LIFE ❖

Not only in Arabia, but in many neighboring civilizations, infanticide was commonly practiced. Pagan Arabs killed their unwanted daughters by burying them alive after birth.

The Koran prohibited this murder:

"You shall not kill your children for fear of want. We will provide for them and for you. To kill them is a great sin."

Koran 17:31

In order to regulate family life, the Koran instituted marriage as a legal agreement, not a sacrament.

The Koran granted the woman rights that had previously been denied her. In marriage, the woman was to receive the dowry herself, to inherit her husband, to own property, and to engage in financial affairs.

The Koran prohibited Muslim women from marrying outside Islam, but it allowed Muslim men to marry Jewish and Christian women. Those wives could retain and practice their faith, but their children were to be raised Muslim.

In order to protect orphaned girls and widows, the Koran permitted polygyny (Koran 4:3), but this was an option, not an injunction, and was strictly predicated on the individual's ability to be just.

A Turkoman *"asmalyk"* used to decorate the bride's camel.

❖ ADHAN ❖

Call to Prayer

The Muslims used to assemble around the Prophet ◗ for prayer. As their numbers grew, there was need to call them together, and the Prophet ◗ chose as the first muezzin (caller to prayer) a slave from Africa. Bilal, who had been freed after accepting Islam, climbed the roof of a house near the mosque which the Prophet ◗ had helped build, and recited the **Adhan.**

To the present day, the muezzin uses these words in his call to prayer:

Allah u Akbar.
God is greater.
God is greater.
I witness that there is no god but God.
I witness that Mohammad is the prophet of God.
Rise to prayer.
Rise to felicity.
God is greater.
God is greater.
There is no god but God.

❖ QIBLA ❖

Direction of Prayer

At the beginning of the revelation, Muslims were invoked to turn in the direction of Jerusalem during prayer. But in Medina, the Koran turned the believers towards the Ka'aba in Mecca (Koran 2:144).

The reason for this change in **Qibla** was the opposition of the Jews to the Prophet ◗ and to the Koranic message. Hereafter, Islamic devotion would focus on the "Sacred Mosque" wherein the Ka'aba is located.

A prayer rug.

❖ TOLERATION ❖

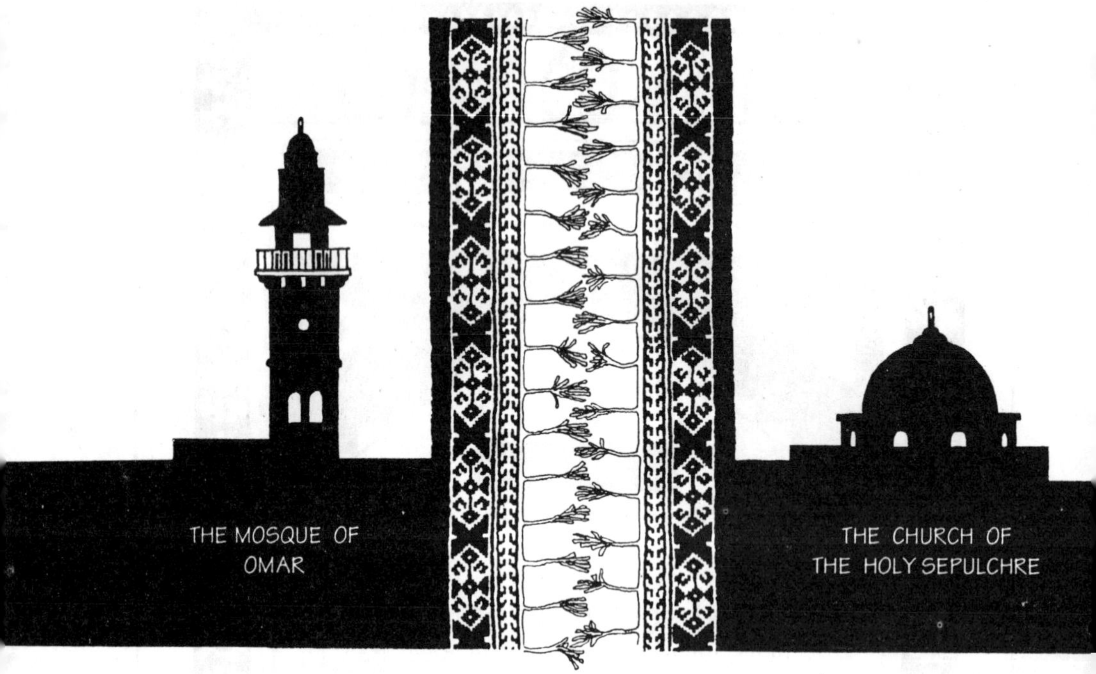

Still the Koran prescribed toleration to the *People of the Book*- the Jews and the Christians. The Koran sanctified God's prophetic revelation to these two communities in the Torah and the New Testament, but accused Jews and Christians of straying from the Straight Path.

The *People of the Book* were part of the Umma and were to be protected in their religious freedom, rights and properties. Because they were not allowed to participate in the military, they were to pay an extra tax.

"There shall be no compulsion in religion."

Koran 2:256

In 635 C.E., the Caliph Omar declined an offer by the Bishop of Jerusalem to pray inside the Church of the Holy Sepulchre lest Muslims build a mosque on that site. He prayed outside where the Mosque of Omar now stands.

The Koran prohibited Muslims from gambling, drinking alcoholic beverages and eating pork.

As these and other laws were being revealed in Medina, the eyes of the Muslims were set on Mecca, mother of the cities (um al-qura, Koran 6:93).

Battles broke out between the Muslims and the polytheists of Mecca. In 630 C.E., the city finally surrendered and the Prophet ◗ triumphantly returned to his birthplace, showing clemency to his former enemies, all of whom now submitted to God.

❖ ❖ ❖

The Prophet ◗ then proceeded to the Ka'aba and destroyed the idols while reciting the Koranic verse:

"Say:

"Truth has come and Falsehood has been overthrown. Falsehood was bound to be discomfited.""

Koran 17:81

Two years later, the Prophet ◗ went to Mecca with over 10,000 followers. This was his last pilgrimage and from Mount Arafat, he gave his farewell address to the Muslims, ending it with these words:

I am leaving you with the Book of God and the Sunnah of his Prophet.
O men, harken well to my words.
Learn that the Muslims constitute one brotherhood.

The Prophet returned to Medina, but in June of that year, 632 C.E., he fell ill, and in the arms of his wife Aisha, daughter of his best friend Abu Bakr, the last of the Prophets of God died. He was 63 years old.

The Prophet ◗
was buried under the floor of Aisha's room in Medina.
A mosque now stands above that spot.

Because his life was steeped in the history of Arabia, Mohammad ◗ has the most accurately documented biography among all the Prophets of monotheism.

Indeed, the historical context of his life underscores the revelation of the **HOLY KORAN.**

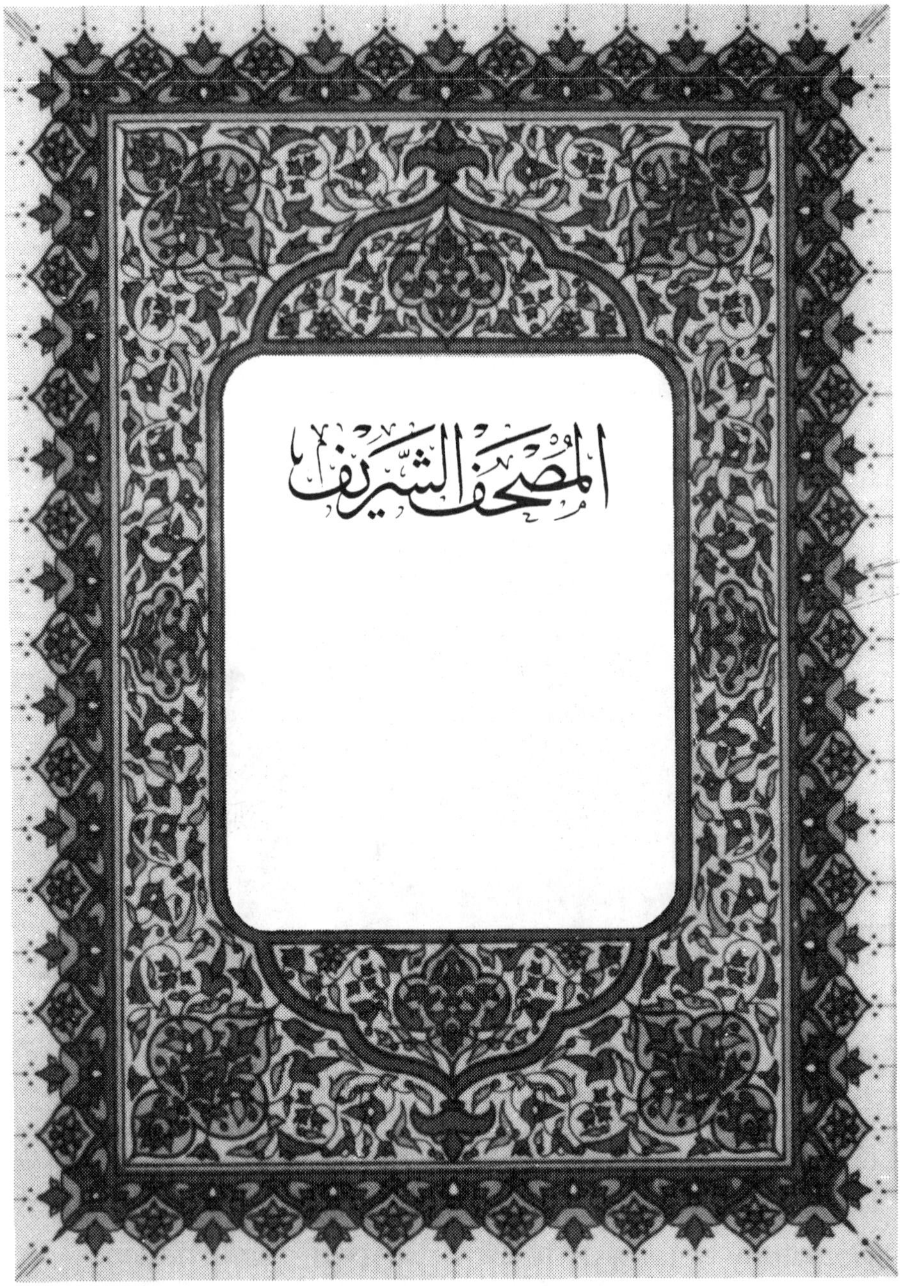

Cover of a Holy Koran.

At the Prophet's ◗ death, Abu Bakr was chosen Caliph, successor to the Prophet ◗. To the Muslims he announced:

O men, if you have been
worshipping Mohammad ◗,
then know that
Mohammad ◗ is dead.
But if you have been
worshipping God,
then know that
God is living and never dies.

This living God was present to the Muslims in the Koran. Throughout his life, the Prophet ◗ had recited the verses of the Koran to the "writers of the revelation" who inscribed the verses on animal skins and bones, flat stones, tablets and tree branches and trunks. Others memorized the divine words.

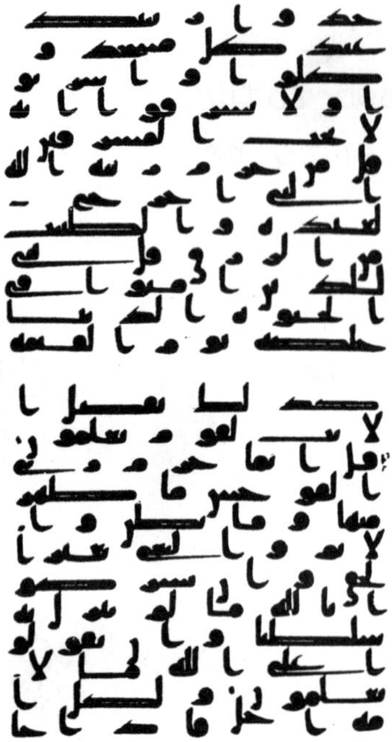

At first, the Koran had neither punctuation nor diacritical marks. These were added in the 1st century A.H.

Abu Bakr (fl. 632-634) realized the need to preserve in a single text the divine words of the Koran just as the Prophet ◗ had recited them.

He authorized Zaid bin Thabit, along with other "Writers" and "Memorizers" to transcribe the Koranic revelation. They only recorded verses that were verified by at least two witnesses who had heard them from the Prophet ◗ himself.

It was, however, the third Caliph, Uthman bin Affan (fl. 644-656) who oversaw the final collation of the text and its streamlining in the Kuraish dialect of Arabic. He then commanded that a few copies of it be made and sent to the centers of the Muslim provinces. Every other version was destroyed, and the Koran has remained absolutely unchanged for 14 centuries.

Uthman's Mushaf (another name for the Koran) is the text still used today. It consists of 114 *surahs* arranged in accordance with the Prophet's ◗ guidance: the longer are at the beginning and then the shorter. Meccan and Medinan revelations are sometimes intermingled, although the former emphasize the theological themes while the latter focus on legislation.

The titles of the *surahs* derive from dominant images or motifs, and a few chapters open with alphabetical letters that remain a divine mystery.

The
Koran
is an exact copy of the words of God which are inscribed in the Celestial Plate. It is thus inerrant.

Although
the
Koran
is in the tradition of other divinely revealed books (Torah, Psalms, Gospels), it supersedes them because it was not corrupted by man. Indeed, only the
Koran
was collected so promptly and meticulously after its prophetic completion.

The
Koran
is the miracle of Islam. It cannot be imitated.

The
Koran
is a revelation in Arabic, but its message is universal.

The
Koran
provides Muslims at all times and in all places with direction in religious and civil duties. It guides them to the

STRAIGHT PATH.
(Koran 1:5)

"He has revealed to you the Book with the Truth, confirming the scriptures which preceded it; for He has already revealed the Torah and the Gospel for the guidance of men, and the distinction between right and wrong."

Koran 3:3

"Say: 'The Holy Spirit brought it (Koran) down from your Lord in truth to reassure the faithful, and to give guidance and good news to those that surrender themselves.' "

Koran 16:102

"Say: "If men and jinn combined to write the like of this Koran, they would surely fail to compose the like, though they helped one another as best they could.' "

Koran 17:88

"We have revealed the Koran in the Arabic tongue that you may understand its meaning. It is a transcript of the eternal book in Our keeping, sublime and full of wisdom."

Koran 43:2-4

ISLAM RESTS ON FIVE PRECEPTS:

◆◆◆◆◆

❖◆◆◆◆

WITNESS: "SHAHADAH"

The essence of Islam is submission to God and admission that Mohammad ◗ is His messenger.

The *Shahadah* in geometric Kufic calligraphy (see page 82 below).

PRAYER: "SALAT"

The Muslim prays five times a day at sunrise, midday, afternoon, sunset and evening. Before prayer, the Muslim prepares by the washing of the head, hands and feet.

Prayer is adoration and gratitude to God. It is for all men and women and can be performed in any unpolluted place facing Mecca. The Muslim can pray alone or with others, although the Friday midday prayer is better in community.

Prayer involves prostration where the forehead touches the ground. Prostration is in acknowledgement of the majesty of God.

◆◆❖◆◆

ALMS: "ZAKAT"

Zakat is prescribed alms. In the Koran, it is always associated with the observation of worship since faith in God is expressed through good deeds. Once a year, the Muslim pays 2 1/2% of his or her capital as alms to the needy.

An advertisement in a Saudi newspaper asking for donations to help Muslim refugees and emigrants in Somalia, Afghanistan and Turkey. Islam (submission) to God enjoined social responsibilty to mankind.

FASTING: "SAWM"

The Muslim fasts for the whole of the month of Ramadan. The fast begins at sunrise ("when a white thread is barely distinguished from a black thread") and ends at sunset.

Throughout, the faster neither eats, drinks, smokes, nor indulges in sexual activity. Children and old people are excused, while the sick and the travelling, along with pregnant women, can postpone their fast until they are fit.

The fast teaches discipline to the soul and recalls for the believer the month in which the first verses of the Koran were revealed. The fast ends on the first day of Shawwal when Muslims celebrate *Eid al-Fitr.*

In many parts of the Middle East, *al-musahharati* roams the streets an hour before the dawn fast begins. By beating on a small drum he awakens people to have their last meal before the fast. The daily fast ends once the muezzin calls for evening prayer.

PILGRIMAGE: "HAJJ"

Once in a lifetime at least, the Muslim should go on pilgrimage to the Ka'aba in Mecca. In that pilgrimage, which is Abrahamic in origin and which stretches between the 7th and the 10th of the month of Dhul Hijja, the last in the Muslim calendar, the believer focuses on the one point in space and time wherein the whole Islamic world acknowledges the might and oneness of God.

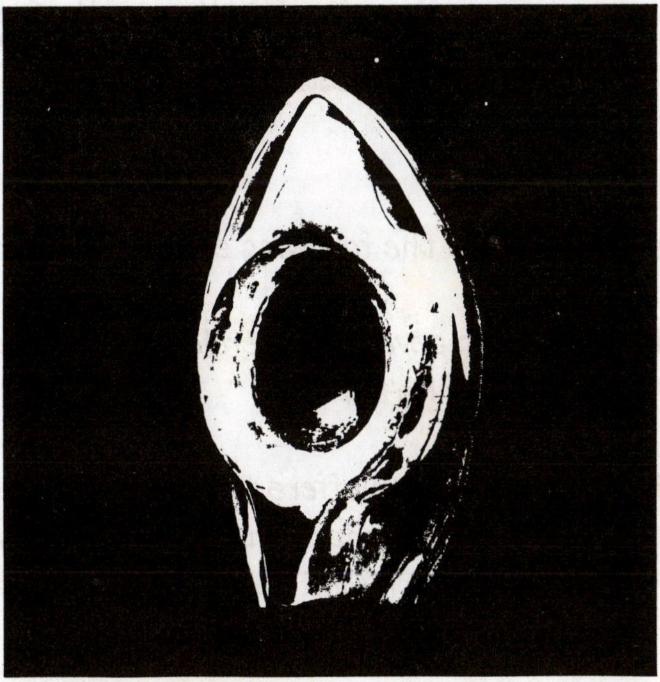

The black stone of the Ka'aba, now encased in silver, has no special properties whatsoever. Muslims salute it only because the Prophet ◗ himself had done so on his final pilgrimage.

During the *Hajj*, pilgrims wear a seamless drape to emphasize human equality before God.

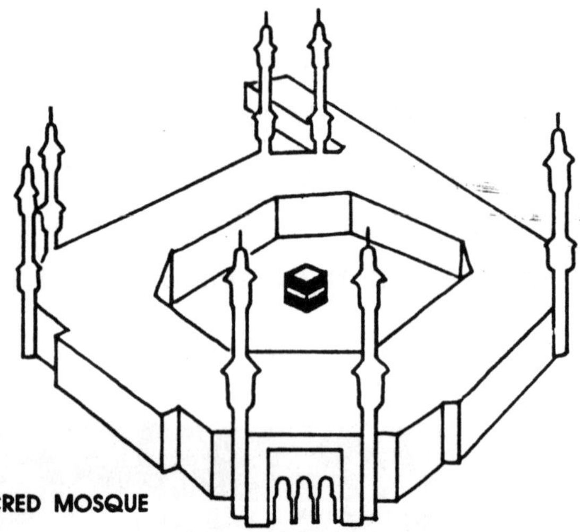

THE SACRED MOSQUE

The *Hajj* involves the following steps:

- The *tawaf*: seven counterclockwise circuits around the Ka'aba.
- The pilgrim then offers two prostrations at the Site of Abraham and goes to the Well of Zamzam (which God had shown to Hajar and her son Ishmael in the desert).
- Afterwards, in recollection of Hajar's patience and perseverance, the pilgrim crosses between the two mountains of Safa and Marwa.

"Lubaika, Allahuma, lubaika",
words which the pilgrim repeats:
"I obey you Lord, I obey".

- He/She then joins the multitude towards the Plain of Arafat and rests there before continuing to Mina to cast stones at three pillars symbolizing the devil.

- Finally, an animal (sheep or camel) is sacrificed and the pilgrim returns to perform the farewell *tawaf* of the Ka'aba.
The meat of the sacrifices is distributed to the poor of the *umma.*

The pilgrimage ends with the Feast of Sacrifice, *Eid al-Adha.* The pilgrim then visits the Prophet's ◗ tomb in Medina.

The Muslim pilgrimage is the largest annual assembly of people on earth. In 1991, nearly two million men and women fulfilled the pilgrimage to Mecca.

The Koran provides a complete vision of God and of human life. During the Prophet's ◗ life and after, however, the Muslims turned to the words, deeds and assents of the Prophet ◗ himself for further guidance on matters alluded to in the Koran.

All that the Prophet ◗ said, did or consented to constitutes the

SUNNA
(the Right Way).

The Sunna is essential for the fulfillment of Muslim life:

for instance, the Koran stipulates ablution and prayer, but it does not describe how the act of ablution is to be conducted. Having observed the Prophet ◗ ablute and then prostrate himself in prayer, the early Muslims imitated him in his SUNNA.

GOD
◆
KORAN
◆
S
U
PROPHET ◗ ◆ N ◆ UMMA
N
A

The SUNNA remains a source of instruction to Muslims today. All the SUNNA is recorded in the Books of HADITH (Traditions of the Prophet ◗).

The SUNNA provides Muslims with the Prophet's ◗ immutable guidance. But it is categorically distinct from the KORAN which is the WORD OF GOD.

The KORAN and the SUNNA constitute al-ASL, the foundation of ISLAM.

All who believe in
ONE
UNIVERSAL
GOD
revealed in the
KORAN

and follow the
SUNNA
of
THE PROPHET
MOHAMMAD

will be rewarded at the
day of judgement with
PARADISE.
All who disobey will be
punished in
HELL.

Koran 83:22-24

The righteous will surely dwell in bliss. Reclining upon soft couches they will gaze around them: and in their faces you shall mark the glow of joy.

Depart into the shadow that will rise high in three columns, giving neither shade nor shelter from the flames, and throwing up sparks as huge as towers, as bright as yellow camels.

Koran 77:30-33

COMMUNITY

"O mankind! We created you from a single soul, male and female, and made you into nations and tribes, so that you may come to know one another. Truly, the most honored of you in God's sight is the greatest of you in piety. God is All-Knowing, All-Aware."

Koran 49:13

■ The spread of Islam was so rapid that within a century after the death of the Prophet ◗ (632), the Muslim faith extended from Spain to China.

Islam was a universal religion that was expressed in Arabic, the language chosen by God for the Koran. As a result, the Muslim relied on Arabic for reciting prayers, naming children, decorating a vase, illuminating a book, or embellishing a dagger-hilt.

The confession of faith in the shape of a boat.

ARABIC READS FROM RIGHT TO LEFT.

Knowledge of Arabic is indispensable to Muslim theologians.

The Reach

Islam stamped five highly-developed civilizations with its own religious character:

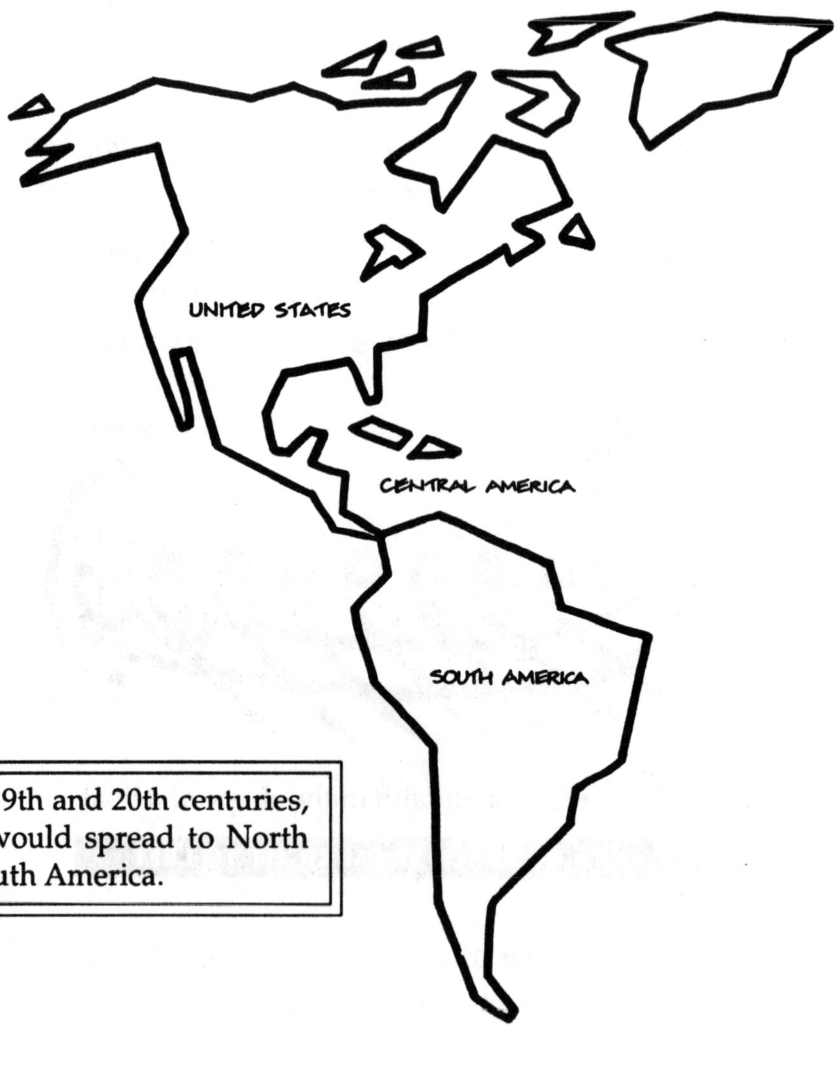

In the 19th and 20th centuries, Islam would spread to North and South America.

# of Islam

The Byzantine,
Persian,
Berber/African,
Turkish, and
Indian civilizations.

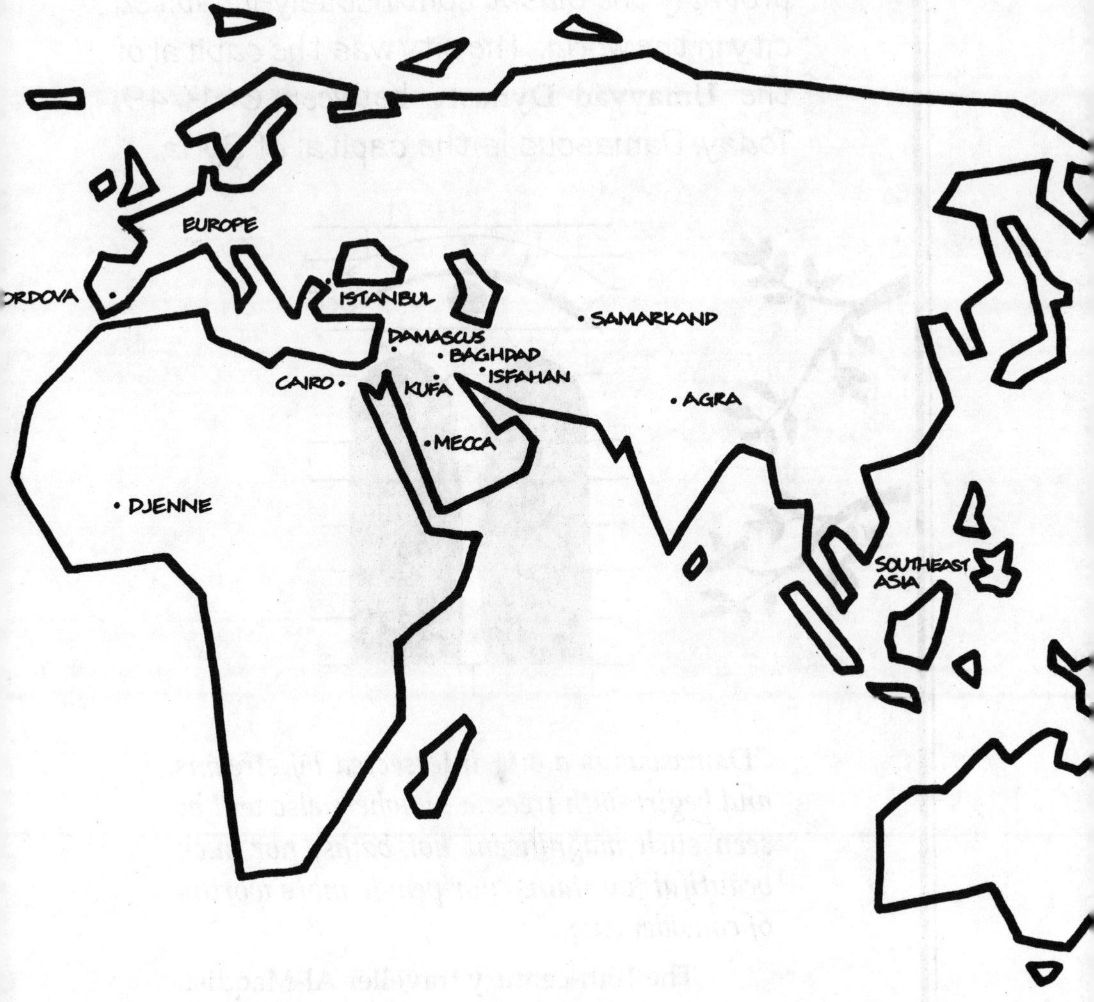

Damascus

The blossoming of Islamic civilization occurred in

❖

DAMASCUS

probably the oldest continuously-inhabited city in the world. The city was the capital of the **Umayyad Dynasty** between 661-749. Today, Damascus is the capital of Syria.

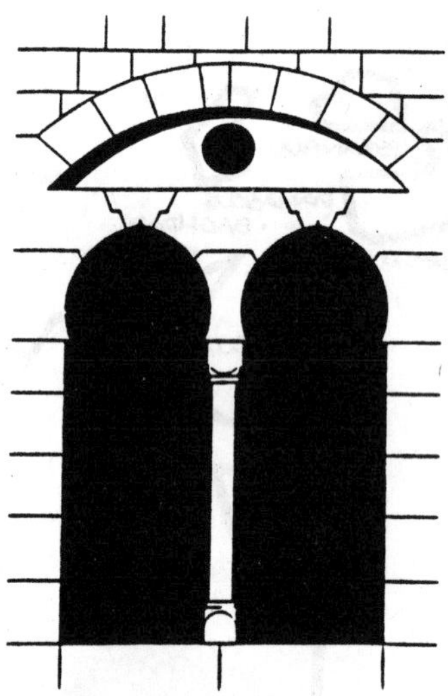

"Damascus is a city intersected by streams and begirt with trees... Nowhere else will be seen such magnificent hot baths, nor such beautiful fountains, nor people more worthy of consideration."

The 10th-century traveller Al-Maqdisi.

A damascene wooden jewelry box inlaid with mother-of-pearl.

Khalid ibn al-Walid, the most capable military strategist in early Islamic history, entered Damascus in 635, after the capitulation of the city.

■ The inhabitants of Damascus did not resist the Muslim conquerors; rather, they supported them against the Byzantine rulers. Indeed, the Bishop of the city regularly brought food to Khalid, the "Sword of Allah."

The latter responded with a benevolent treaty:

> *In the name of God the merciful, the compassionate.*
> *This is what Khalid would grant the inhabitants of Damascus when he enters it.*
> *He shall grant them security for their lives, properties and churches.*
> *Their city wall shall not be demolished, neither shall any Muslim be quartered in their homes.*
> *So long as they pay poll-tax, nothing but good shall befall them.*

Trans. Philip Hitti.

Islam was putting to practice the toleration and coexistence which the Koran preached:

> *"And if they incline to peace, incline you too to it, and trust in God. Lo! He is the Hearer, the Knower."*
>
> *Koran 8:61*

As Damascus ruled the Muslim world, Islamic culture moved closer to the Hellenized Mediterranean and away from the desert.

In Damascus, the Islamic institution gave rise to the

FIRST COIN STRUCK IN ISLAM

FIRST POSTAL SERVICE IN ISLAM

FIRST RECORDS OFFICE IN ISLAM

FIRST REGULAR ARMY IN ISLAM

FIRST MOSQUE OUTSIDE THE ARABIAN PENINSULA

■ The courtyard of the Prophet's ◗ house in Medina served as the first mosque, the concept of which developed over the years to include additional features. These can be found in the **Umayyad Mosque** in Damascus, a fine example of the

❖ COMMUNITY MOSQUE ❖

With the spread of Islam, mosques adapted to indigenous traditional architecture, resulting in a variety of styles. Whether Arabic or Iranian, Turkish, Indian or African, a Muslim House of Worship will always share the principles of the Umayyad Mosque.

The Umayyad Mosque, Damascus, built 706-715.

In Islam, the building of a mosque is an act of great merit. The Prophet ◗ said in the *Hadith:* *"Whoever builds a mosque, desiring thereby God's pleasure, God builds for him the like of it in paradise."*

The mosque is designed to create a space of serenity, rather than exaltation.

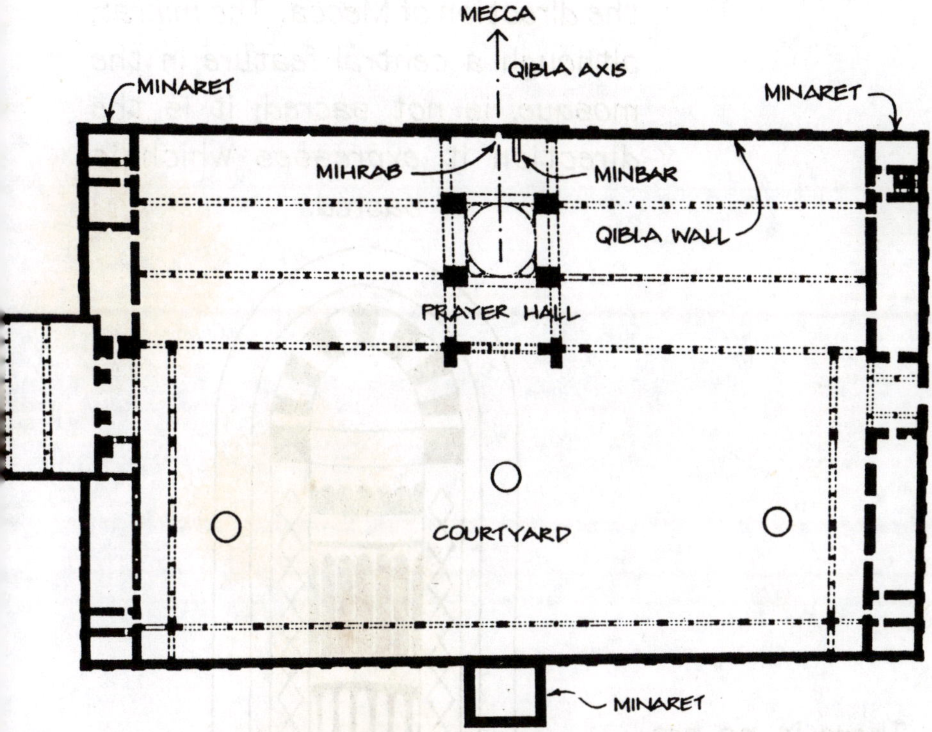

Plan of the Umayyad Mosque, Damascus.

Islam discouraged the portrayal of human and animal forms for fear of idolatry. The Muslims turned their artistic imagination towards the abstract, decorating their mosques with geometrical patterns, arabesques and the calligraphy (beautiful handwriting) of Koranic verses.

During prayer, worshippers form long rows facing the Qibla wall.

The ❖ MIHRAB ❖ refuge

a niche within that wall, emphasizes the direction of Mecca. The *mihrab*, although a central feature in the mosque, is not sacred; it is the direction it expresses which is sacred.

There is no processional worship in Islam. The rectangular shape of the Prayer Hall fulfills the worshippers' need to pray as close to the Qibla wall (hence, Mecca) as possible. Neither are there any priests in Islam: holiness resides solely in God and the Koran, and not in any special individual or class of persons. Even the Prophet ◗ is viewed as just a simple human being, with no supernatural qualities (Koran 3:144-145).

To the right of the *mihrab* stands

the
❖ MINBAR ❖
pulpit

which consists of narrow steps enclosed by hand-rails and leading to a platform often covered by a canopy. It is from this *minbar* that the Friday noon sermon is delivered, Friday being Islam's holy day (Koran 62:9).

When the Imam (leader of the prayer) stands to preach, he never occupies the top step of the *minbar*. That is always left empty in recognition of the Prophet's ◗ pre-eminence.

Because there is no separation between secular and religious life in Islam, the sermon addresses social, political, international and doctrinal matters.

A fundamental feature of the mosque is the

❖——COURTYARD——❖

which precedes the prayer hall and accommodates the overflow of worshippers. The removal of shoes is required prior to entering the mosque precinct; the worshipper then performs the ablution ritual at the fountain generally located in the courtyard.

Devotional and ordinary activities meet in the courtyard of the mosque. There the community can pray, while students can learn, travellers can rest, merchants can negotiate and the weary can find peace in God.

In the larger mosques, the courtyard may be surrounded by an **arcade,** *riwaq* in Arabic. This word literally means "composure" for contemplation and learning. The rhythmic arcades help bring the scale of the large prayer halls down to a human level. In the shade of the *riwaq,* many a teacher in Islam has taught the principles of faith, for the mosque is a place of worship, of sanctuary and of study.

allows the muezzin to call the believers to prayer. In small communities, he chants the words himself; in large cities, loudspeakers are used and the call is synchronized among all the mosques. In nearly all Islamic countries, the call to prayer is in Arabic.

The structure of the minaret often reveals the geographic location of the mosque: the minaret is square in Spain and North Africa, round with a conical cap in Turkey, composite in Egypt, and sometimes octagonal and capped with a dome in India.

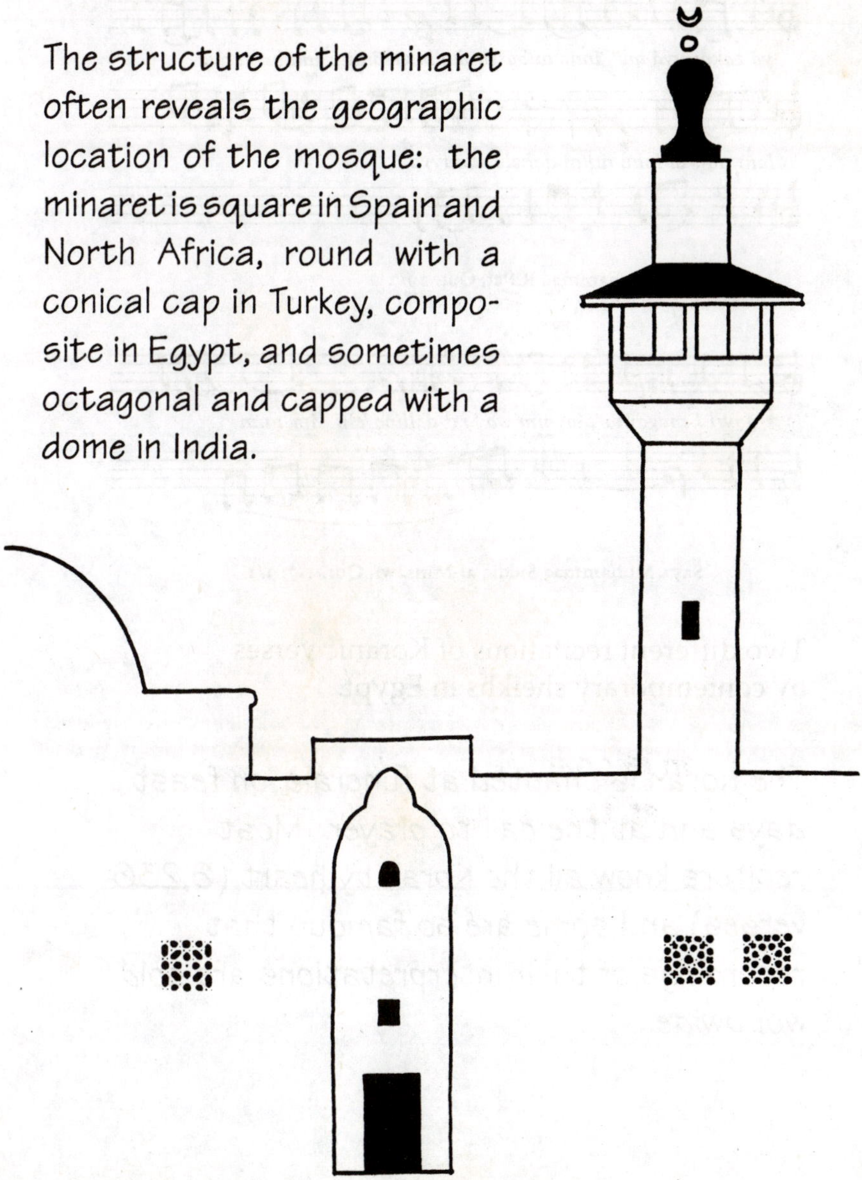

When the muezzin recites the Koran, he follows established melodic cadences known as

❖ TAJWEED ❖

Tajweed or chanting brings God's revelation into the affective experience of the believer. The Koran is to be felt as well as understood.

Šayx Muḥammad Rifʿat, Qur. 19/7

Šayx Muḥammad Ṣiddīq al-Minšāwī, Qur. 1/7, 2/1

Two different recitations of Koranic verses by contemporary sheikhs in Egypt.

The Koran is chanted at funerals, on feast days and at the call to prayer. Most reciters know all the Koran by heart (6,236 verses) and some are so famous that recordings of their interpretations are sold worldwide.

the spiritual equals of men (Koran 4:1), also worship at the mosque. Decency, however, dictates a private quarter for them, and when such a quarter is not found, women pray in rows behind men. At the mosque, as well as in public spaces, women cover their heads and arms. The facial veil found in some Muslim countries is not a Koranic injunction, but a local custom.

One of the *Hadiths* of the Prophet ◗ stated:

"Do not prohibit the handmaids of God from attending the mosques of God."

The Prophet ◗ invoked men to be gentle to their spouses:

"The most perfect in faith amongst believers is he who is best in manner and kindest to his wife."

Women were always active in communal and military affairs. In 656, the Prophet's ◗ wife Aisha took part in the Battle of the Camel (so named because the battle centered around the camel she rode). Aisha was later buried in the Umayyad mosque.

Women were also intellectually active: Aisha was well-versed in Arabic poetry and genealogy. After the death of the Prophet ◗, she became an authority on the Sunna, so much so, that over 200 authentic *Hadiths* are ascribed to her.

Kufa

Calligraphy and theological studies in Islam focus on the Koran.

The first calligraphic style (*Kufi*) and the foundations of legal studies were begun in

◆

KUFA

a city in Iraq.

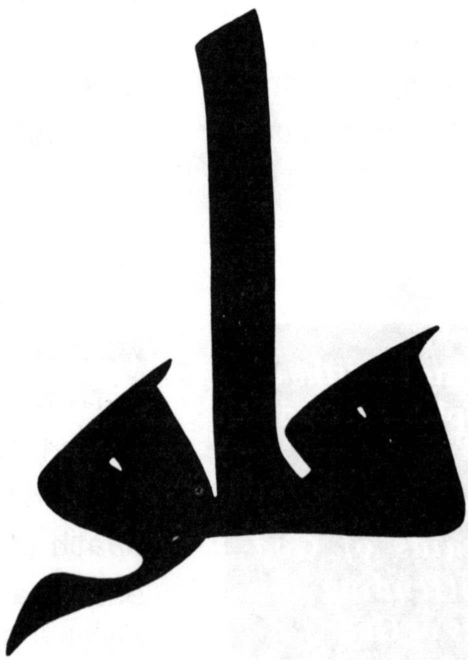

"If you seek elegance, go to Kufa."
The 10th-century writer al-Jahiz.

To the Muslims, copying the Koran, the written Word of God, is an act of deep devotion, for in Islam, art is not separate from faith.

The *Kufi* script, which borrows its name from the city of Kufa, is angular, geometric and monumental.

The *Naskhi* calligraphic style, a rounded, cursive, easily legible script, was later introduced. These are but two of the numerous styles of calligraphy that developed as a reflection of the geographical diversity of the Islamic peoples.

■ By expanding outside its Arabian boundaries, Islam faced new social, legal and religious issues that had not earlier challenged it. To resolve these issues,

◆ FOUR SCHOOLS OF LAW ◆
fiqh

appeared, representing different approaches to
***Ijtihad*: Theological Reasoning.**

1. HANAFI SCHOOL

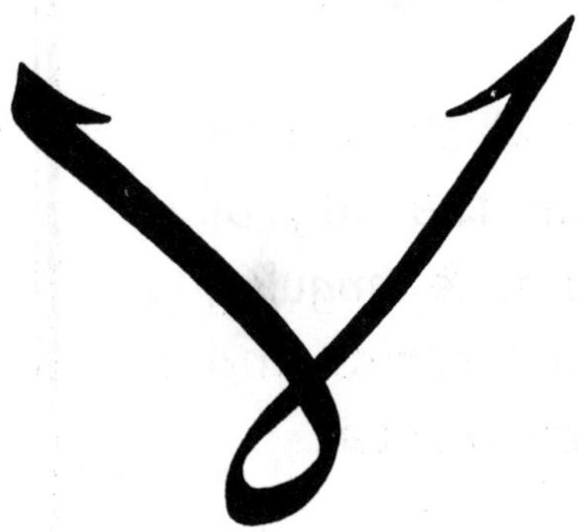

Founded by **Abu Hanifa** (699-767) who lived and died in Kufa. He urged that free reason serve as the principal conduit to Islamic interpretation. Thus his became the **School of Opinion.**

2. MALIKI SCHOOL

Founded by **Malik ibn Anas** (710-795) who lived in Medina. He rejected free reason and emphasized that the Traditions of the Prophet ◗ (*Hadith*) should alone guide the Muslim. His became the **School of Tradition.**

3. SHAFI'I SCHOOL

Founded by **Mohammad ibn Idris al-Shafi'i** (767-820) whose major work *Risala* established for Sunni Islam the **Foundations of Jurisprudence.**

If there is a legal problem, the Muslim should try to solve it by first referring to the **Koran**; if there is no definite answer, he should turn to the **Sunna**; if there is still no answer, turn to the **concensus** of the whole community; and as a final recourse, draw an **analogy** with the **Koran**.

For instance: alcoholic beverage is prohibited in the Koran, but there is no mention of hard drugs. Since alcohol is prohibited because of its intoxicating effect, and since hard drugs generate a similar effect, then by analogy, hard drugs are also prohibited.

4. HANBALI SCHOOL

Ahmad ibn Hanbal (780-855) lived and lectured in Baghdad. For him only the **Koran** and the **Sunna** guided the Muslim.

Muslim calligraphers turned words into shapes: fruits (apples and pears) and animals (birds and lions) infused language with visual impact.

These Schools of Law have moulded the intellectual life of Islam. There has never been a conflict between them because they fully accept each other's rules and practices.
Followers of these legal schools constitute nearly 85% of the Muslim umma.

They are the
◆ SUNNIS ◆
(followers of the Sunna in the Books of *Hadith*).

The compilation of *Hadith* was undertaken by the Persian jurist **al-Bukhari** (810-870) who produced the <u>Definitive</u> (*Sahih*) edition. Out of the 600,000 sayings that he gathered (and partly memorized), he identified only 7,275 as authentic Prophetic sayings.

A Selection from al-Bukhari's *Hadith*

On Charity,
the Prophet ◗ said:

"The man who exerts himself on behalf of the widow and the poor one is like the one who struggles in the way of God, or the one who keeps awake at night for prayer and fasts during the day."

On Faith:

"None of you has faith unless he loves for his brother what he loves for himself."

On Work:

"No one eats better food than that which he eats out of the work of his hands."

On Hospitality:

"A man should accompany his guest to the door of the house."

On Knowledge:

"The learned ones are the heirs of the Prophets- they leave knowledge as their inheritance; he who inherits it inherits a great fortune."

The ◆ SHI'ITES ◆ were the Party (*shi'a*) of Ali bin Abi Taleb

the fourth Caliph to rule the Muslim community (fl. 656-661). His *Shi'a* believed that he should have been the first Caliph; they also believed that after him came eleven **Imams,** the last of whom went into occultation in 874, but would appear again at the end of time as the **Mahdi** (the chosen one) to bring justice to the world.

Each of the twelve Imams had divine powers which made him **infallible** in legal judgement; thus the Imam alone could rule the *Umma.*

The lion was the symbol of Ali. This is a calligraphic rendering of a prayer of praise to Ali.

Although Ali played a chief role in Shi'ite spirituality, the two Imams who formulated Shi'ite law were **Mohammad Baqir** (677-733) and **Ja'far as-Sadik** (702-765).

■ Ali was murdered in Kufa in 661, and his followers called upon his eldest son **Hasan**, the second Imam, to become Caliph. He was later succeeded by his brother **Hussein,** as the third Imam. As Hussein marched from Medina to Kufa, he and his family were cut down by the Umayyad Ruler **Yazid** in the field of **Karbala,** northwest of Kufa. Every 10th of *Moharram*, the Shi'ites mourn the death of Hussein and lament their failure to assist him.

The names of the twelve Imams.

From Shi'ism many sects emerged that are present today. They include: the Zaidis, Ismailis, Agha Khanis, Druzes, and Alawites.

> **Both Sunnis and Shi'ites recognize the primacy of the Koran and the Sunna. In deciding matters outside those sources, however, the Sunnis depend on community concensus while the Shi'ites rely on the infallibility of the Imams.**

The meticulous scholarship used in the collection of the Koran and of the *Hadith* produced a number of theological sciences crucial to Islamic

◆ TAFSEER ◆

Exegesis

1. **The Science of the Contexts of Revelation:**
   This science focused on the historical circumstances in which the verses of the Koran were revealed. To master this science, jurists had to learn the exact dialect of Arabic used by Kuraish, the Prophet's ◗ tribe.

2. **The Science of Meccan and Medinan Verses** (Historical Criticism):
   The jurists studied the gradual stages of Koranic revelation. This science examined chronology, geography, thematic unity, and biographical history.

The Science of Abrogation:

In the Koran, *God* abrogated certain commands. For example, wine was condemned and prohibited (Koran 2:219; 5:90). Jurists had to learn the reasons governing the divine abrogations.

The Science of the Reputation of Transmitters:

Because the compilation of the Koran and later of the *Hadith* depended on oral and written transmissions, there was need to verify the reliability of transmitters in order to arrive at an accurate text and pronunciation. Thus the study of the transmitters' reputation, biography and genealogy.

In Kufa lived the first Arab alchemist,

◆ **JABIR BIN HUNAYN** ◆
(fl. 760-815)

known in the West as **Geber,**
"King of the Arabs".

Alchemy had a special place in Islamic science because it used experimentation to test the speculative theories on the nature of the universe. In so doing, alchemists shared the concerns of theologians who sought to discover the divine order in the creation.

Jabir's writings and experiments, along with the work of his disciples, transmitted the knowledge of the mineral acids to the Western World. From the Arabic word for "alchemy" came the word "chemistry".

A 15th-century German illustration of the world's major alchemists: Geber, Arnold, ar-Razi (see page 102 below), and Hermes.

Baghdad

In the 9th and 10th centuries, the greatest city in Islam and the world's center of learning was

❖

BAGHDAD

It was built in 762 by the **Caliph al-Mansur** and became the capital of the **Abbasid Dynasty**. Baghdad is the capital of Iraq.

"Among the cities of the world, Baghdad stands out as the professor of the community of Islam."

The geographer Yaqut in 1228.

The circular plan of the city demonstrated the centralization of power in the hands of the ruler.

None of the structures below survived the Mongol invader Hulako in 1258.

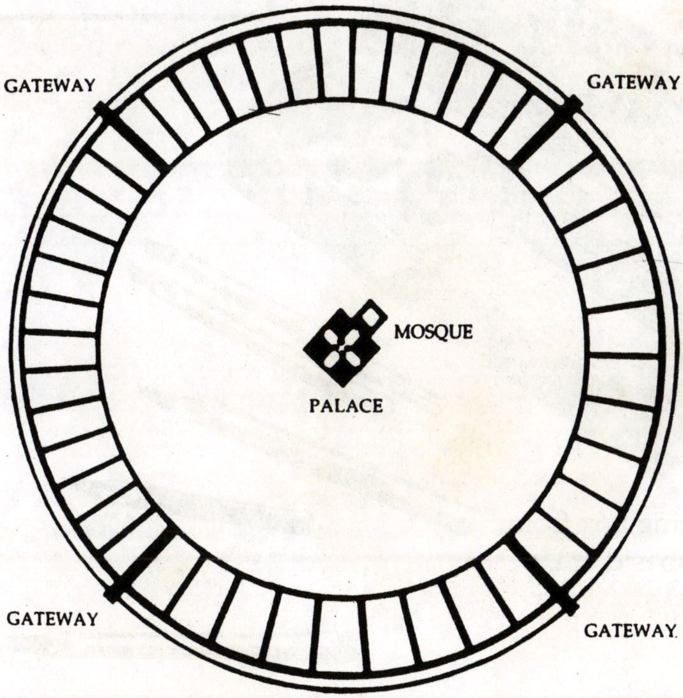

■ It was in Baghdad that Islam came in contact with the civilizations of Persia, India and China.

The Muslims learned the art of **Paper Production** from Chinese papermakers captured in a battle fought in 751. Less than half a century later, the Barmicide family built the first paper mill in Baghdad.

Only in the 13th century did the Europeans learn the use of paper from the Muslims.

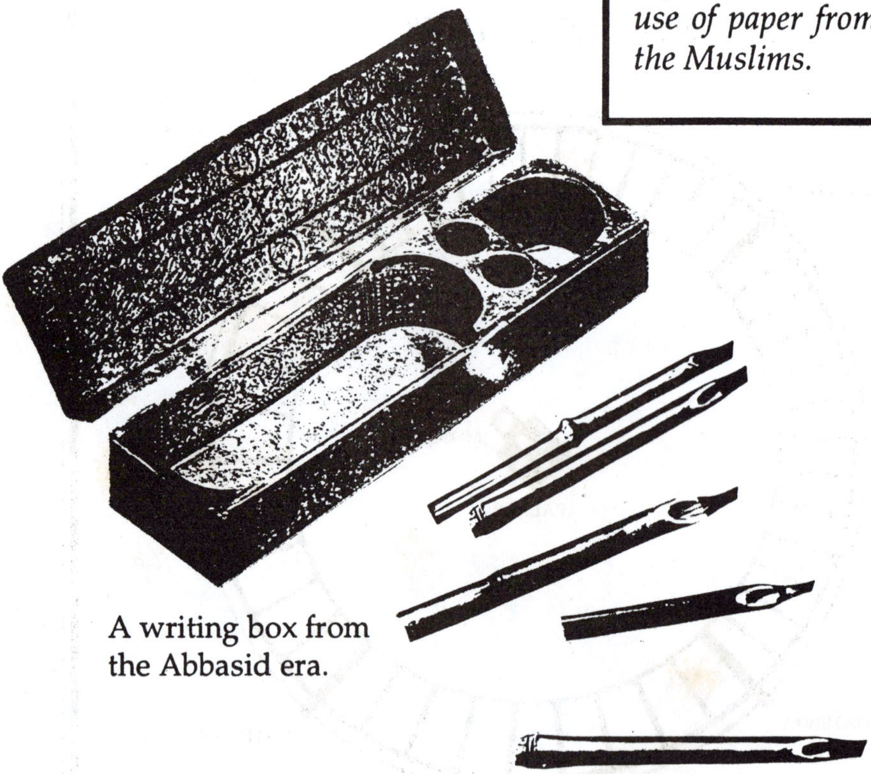

A writing box from the Abbasid era.

The Muslim developed a unique sensitivity for ink colors. A handbook by an 11th-century Tunisian writer lists ruby-red, purple, green, and yellow colors along with shades of peacock-hue, rose, pistachio, and apricot.

The supreme achievement of Baghdad was the

❖ HOUSE OF WISDOM ❖

established by the Caliph **al-Ma'moon** (fl. 813-833) to oversee translations of books on mathematics, astronomy and medicine- three areas in which Muslim scientists excelled. The "House" served as a Library, a Center for Translation and Manuscript Copying, and as a Research Laboratory and Observatory.

Story has it that al-Ma'moon hesitated to build the "House" until he had a dream in which Aristotle urged him on.

And he obeyed.

■ Muslims, Christians, Jews, Zoroastrians, Sabaeans and Hindus harmoniously cooperated in research at the "House".

Translations from Persian, Greek, Syriac and Sanskrit led to the coining and Arabization of new words, many of which have found their way into the English language.

Words of purely Arabic origin have also enriched the English vocabulary, among them:

Implements:
alembic
carafe
jar
mattress
sofa

Colors:
azure
crimson

Astronomy:
almanac
nadir
rocket
zenith

Foods:
apricot
artichoke
banana
candy
coffee
lemon
orange
saffron
sugar

Animals:
baboon
gazelle
giraffe

In Spanish, there are nearly 6,500 words of Arabic/Persian derivation.

Miscellaneous:
carat
cipher
hazard

Medical terms:
alcohol
camphor
soda
syrup
talisman

Elements:
alkali
amber
arsenic
benzine
borax
elixir

Military Terms:
admiral
arsenal
assassin
cable
magazine

In the House of Wisdom, the first original treatise on Algebra was written by a Zoroastrian scientist who had converted to Islam

❖ AL-KHAWARIZMI ❖
(780-850)

The word "algebra" which entered the English language in the 1500's derives from the Arabic *al-jabr*, which was Khawarizmi's operation of "binding together" equations and . . . bones.

The binding of bones, from a medical text of the 14th century.

Al-Khawarizmi was the first mathematician to use numerals instead of letters. The translation of his work into Latin in the 12th century introduced the "Arabic" numerals and the Zero (from Arabic *sifr*) to the West and made possible the beginnings of European mathematics.

The Muslims adopted two

❖ NUMERICAL SYSTEMS ❖

from India. The first was used in the western part of the Islamic Empire and remains in use today in the Arab world:

٩ ٨ ٧ ٦ ٥ ٤ ٣ ٢ ١ ٠

The second was used in the eastern part. The Muslims referred to these numbers as "Indian"; upon their adoption in Europe, they became known as Arabic numerals.

9 8 7 6 5 4 3 2 1 0

Islam advocated the study of arithmetic, geometry and physics because these sciences helped the theologians in relating human motivation and action to the divine will.

Science clarified the mysteries of God's creation.

The greatest physician of the medieval world

was

❖ **AR-RAZI** ❖

(865-952)

known in Latin as Rhazes.

After living in Baghdad, he returned to his native city of Rayy, in Persia, and headed the hospital there.

Long before the discovery of bacteria, ar-Razi knew the importance of hygiene: to choose a site for a hospital in Baghdad, he hung pieces of meat at various points around the city. He recommended that the hospital be built at the location where the meat had putrefied the slowest.

Surgical instruments used in the 10th century.

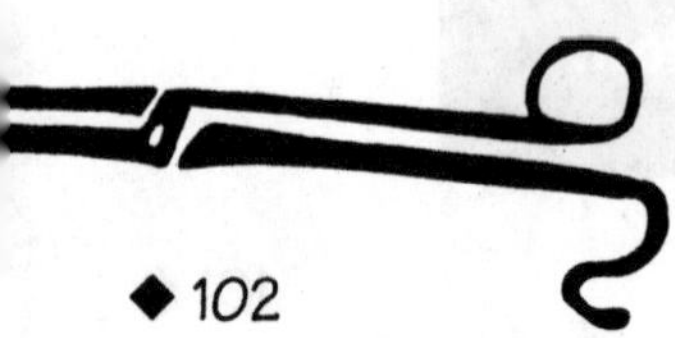

Muslims were encouraged towards medicine by the emphasis on ritual purity and physical cleanliness in the Koran and the *Hadith*.

From Isfahan, east of Baghdad, came another Persian doctor, the "Prince of Physicians",

❖ IBN SINA ❖

Avicenna

(980-1037)

He was a precocious boy who had memorized all the Koran by the time he was ten.

In close to 1,000,000 words, Ibn Sina's <u>Canon of Medicine</u> systematized the medical sciences of the Egyptians, the Greeks, the Romans, the Persians, the Indians, and the Arabs. From the 12th to the 17th century, it was the chief text used in European medical universities.

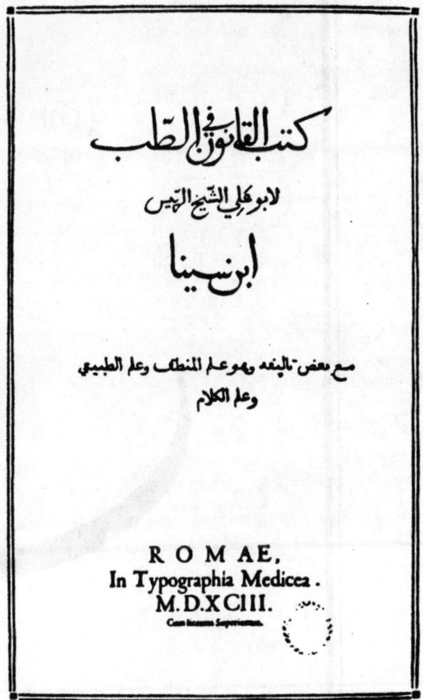

كتب القانون في الطب

لابو علي الشيخ الرئيس

ابن سينا

مع بعض تاليفه وهو علم المنطق وعلم الطبيعي

وعلم الكلام

ROMAE,
In Typographia Medicea.
M.D.XCIII.
Cum licentia Superiorum.

The Canon published in Rome, 1593.

Ibn Sina wrote about surgery, but it was in Muslim Spain, where religious authorities permitted dissection, that Islamic surgery reached its highest standard.

Cordova

Many physicians were philosophers and the Muslim university curriculum listed medicine and philosophy under the single heading of *hikma* (wisdom).

The great center of wisdom in the West was

✦

CORDOVA

in Andalusia
(the Muslim name of Spain).

Andalusian
Maghribi script.

"He grants wisdom to whom He pleases; and he to whom wisdom is granted receives indeed a benefit overflowing."

Koran 2:269

"Scientists and poets flocked to Cordova, while writers and soldiers mingled with the noble and the learned... From Cordova shone light unto the world."

The 12th-century Andalusian historian al-Hijari.

Cordova in the 12th century

POPULATION: 500,000
(Paris 40,000)
MOSQUES: 700
BATHS: 300
(Englishmen condemned their use as pagan.)
LIBRARIES: 70
UNIVERSITY HOLDINGS: 400,000 books.
(The university of Paris had one tenth that amount.)
STREETS: Paved.
(Oxford students waded in mud.)
RELIGIONS:
Islam, Christianity and Judaism.
(Nowhere else in Europe was there similar coexistence.)

■ Islam encouraged philosophical speculation within the limits of religious faith. Muslims examined the place of the rational thinker in a society ruled by divine law and revelation, and the relationship of theology to philosophy.

Ever since the days of Damascus, Muslim philosophers had been studying Greek sources, particularly Plato and Aristotle. Indeed, it was through the Muslims of Andalusia that the writings of Aristotle entered Christian Europe.

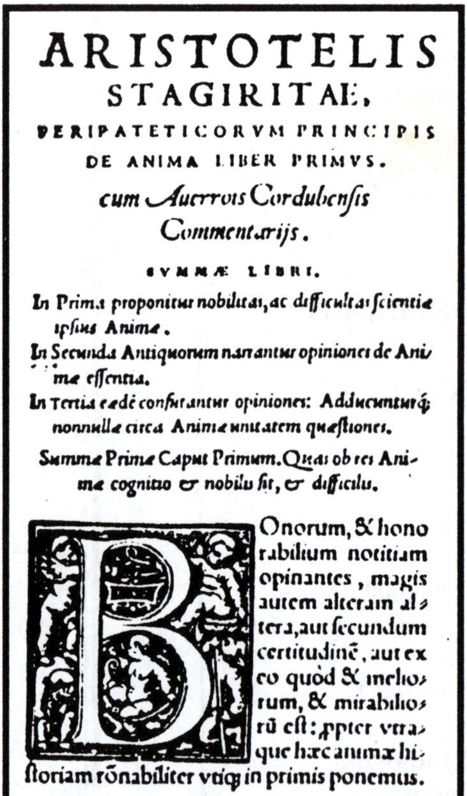

ARISTOTELIS STAGIRITAE, PERIPATETICORVM PRINCIPIS DE ANIMA LIBER PRIMVS.

cum Auerrois Cordubensis Commentarijs.

SVMMAE LIBRI.

In Prima proponitur nobilitas, ac difficultas scientiae ipsius Animae.

In Secunda Antiquorum narrantur opiniones de Animae essentia.

In Tertia eadē confutantur opiniones: Adducunturq; nonnullae circa Animae unitatem quaestiones.

Summae Primae Caput Primum. Quas ob res Animae cognitio & nobilis sit, & difficilis.

BOnorum, & honorabilium notitiam opinantes, magis autem alteram altera, aut secundum certitudinē, aut ex eo quòd & meliorum, & mirabiliorū est: ꝓpter vtraque haec animae historiam rōnabiliter vtiq; in primis ponemus.

From Aristotle's treatise on the soul with the commentary of Averroes (16th century).

✦ IBN RUSHD ✦

Averroes

(1126-1198)

oversaw the translation of Aristotle from Greek into Arabic and wrote over 38 commentaries on the Greek philosopher. After their translation into Latin, Ibn Rushd's writings so dominated the medieval Scholasticism of Europe that in 1223, the University of Paris banned "Averroism" from its curriculum.

Few heeded the ban since, to the medieval student, Ibn Rushd was "The Commentator" on Aristotle "The Philosopher".

"The School of Athens", by Raphael, the Italian Renaissance painter.
Ibn Rushd is in the turban.

Ibn Rushd believed that Aristotelian philosophy and Koranic theology were "twin sisters"- a view which Muslim theologians later firmly rejected.

One of Ibn Rushd's disciples was the Jewish thinker

✦ MUSA IBN MAYMOON ✦
Maimonides

who introduced Averroism into Judaism.

Like other Jewish writers in Andalusia, Ibn Maymoon wrote in Arabic and closely followed the teachings of his mentor.

It is in Muslim Spain that the Jews produced their greatest poetry, philosophy and sciences since the first century C.E.

Although Aristotelian philosophy was suppressed by religious orthodoxy, Islamic philosophy as "Wisdom of Illumination" continued in Persia. But instead of dealing with the classical subjects of form and matter, the philosophers turned to theosophy and Sufism.

In the Andalusia of philosophers,

✦ ARABESQUE AND GEOMETRIC ✦ PATTERNS

attained great beauty.

Arabesque patterns are based on highly-stylized vegetal motifs, while geometric patterns rely on the juxtaposition of regular polygons (triangles, squares and hexagons). These abstract elements are repeated infinitely to create a uniform field of decoration.

Whether embellishing a bowl, carving a wooden *minbar* or tiling a mosaic floor, arabesque and geometric patterns, in their harmony and unity, convey the infinity and indivisibility of God.

Arabesque is man's discovery of God. That is why the Muslim artist never signed his work, whether on stone, tile, wood, plaster, metal, textile, or miniature.

Isfahan

Muslim philosophers often crossed paths and pens with mystics and Sufis. The Sufi poet **Jalal ul-Din ar-Rumi** (1207-1273) lived for a few years in the city of

❖

ISFAHAN

in Iran.

I sought a soul in the sea,
And found a coral there;
Beneath the foam for me
An ocean was all laid bare.

Into my heart's night
Along a narrow way
I groped: and lo! the light,
An infinite land of day.

Trans. A.J. Arberry.

In the 16th century, Isfahan became the capital of the **Safavid Empire.**

The greatest poets of Sufism in Islam were Persian and the most famous among them came from Isfahan, Shiraz, Tibriz, and Naisapur. Typical of their social mobility was Rumi: born a Persian in Balkh (Afghanistan), he travelled to Aleppo (Syria), lived briefly in Isfahan then settled in Konya (Turkey) where he died. He was buried in the garden of the Sultan who was one of his disciples.

■ The word "Sufi" probably derives from the Arabic *Suf* which means wool. Sufis wore wool in order to demonstrate their rejection of luxury. The Prophet ◗ had said:

"Do not wear silk or silk brocade, and do not drink in vessels of gold and silver, and do not eat in bowls made of them; for they are for them in this life and for us in the next."

A wandering Sufi. (17th century)

Through the exercise of silence, solitude, hunger, and wakefulness, the Sufis attained the gnosis of God. They also meditated on the Prophet Mohammad ◗ as the "Divine Light of Illumination". Thus taught the Andalusian Sufi **Ibn Arabi** (1165-1240), known as the "Great Master", who met Rumi in Damascus.

Rumi spent 40 years composing his poem, the *Methnawi.* He opened it with a reference to the **Nay** (Flute), the musical instrument which symbolizes the soul after its separation from God.

The followers of Rumi's *Tariqa* (Sufi path) used music and dance in their quest of divine oneness. They are the **Whirling Dervishes.** (Dervish is Persian for "poor").

Pivoting on one foot as they circle--right hand facing heaven, left hand facing earth--the dancers symbolize spinning planets revolving about God.

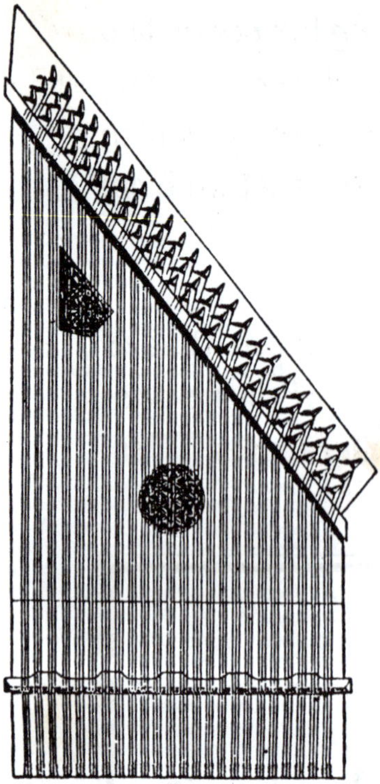

Two of the greatest theoreticians of music in Islam were **Abul Faraj al-Isfahani** (who came from Isfahan) and his contemporary, the Turkish Sufi

❖ AL-FARABI ❖
(870-950)

Al-Farabi is credited with the invention of the viol and the development of the Babylonian instrument, *al-Qanoon.*

From Islam, the West developed the **rebec** from the *rabab,* the **timbel** from the *tabel* and the **lute** from *al-oud* (Arabic for wood).

Although the Koran has no explicit pronouncements on music, some jurists condemned it as frivolous and sinful. The Sufis, however, emphasized that in an appropriate context, music served as a vehicle for spiritual illumination.

"Listening to music has a divine effect that moves the heart to Allah. He who listens to it spiritually attains to Him, but he who listens sensually falls into heresy."

The Sufi writer Dhu'l Noon (d. 860).

Central to the Sufis was the Koran with its imagery of light (24: 4-5) and of the "veil" which separates God's splendor from the eyes of man. The life of the Prophet ◗ and the Hijra also inspired the Sufis who saw their own quest of God as a journey ending with the beatific vision.

One of the earliest Sufis in Islam was a woman from Basra, **Rabi'a al-'Adawiyya** (d. 801) who wrote the following prayer:

"O God!
If I worship You in fear of Hell,
burn me in it;
and if I worship You in hope of Paradise,
exclude me from it;
but if I worship You for Your own being,
do not withhold from me
Your everlasting beauty."

In the 16th century, the Sufi followers of Rumi constructed **clocks** in order to regulate the time of prayer; they also used the Rosary in their meditations. From Mecca to Samarkand, the Sufis used the **99-bead rosary** to recite the 99 names of God in the Koran.

Samarkand

In

✱

SAMARKAND

the Mongolian king **Timurlane** (Timur the lame) built a city *"whose shining turrets dismayed the heavens and cast the fame of Ilion's tower to hell."*

(Christopher Marlowe, English playwright.)

Samarkand is in the heart of Asia and became the cultural center of Eastern Islam after the fall of Baghdad.

Timurlane pushed Islam westward towards Moscow and eastward towards the Indian Ganges river. His grandson, **Ulugh Beg**, built one of the finest observatories (1420-1437) in Islamic history.

The observatory had a large arc with which the altitude of the celestial bodies could be measured.

"It was He that gave the sun his brightness and the moon her light, ordaining her phases that you may learn to compute the seasons and the years."

Koran 10:5

In Islam, the study of nature is part of religious life, and there is no contradiction between faith and scientific inquiry.

■ Muslims specifically studied astronomy and charted constellations in order to identify the direction of the Qibla, the beginning of the lunar year and the time of prayer. Their research was inspired by the Koran's many references to astronomy.

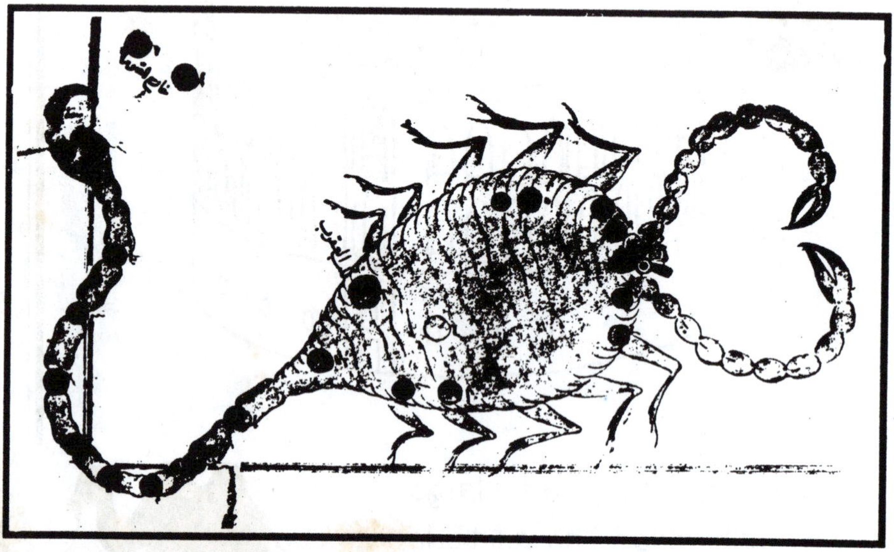

The constellation *Acrab,* from the Arabic for "scorpion".

Omar Khayyam (d. 1123), famous for his poems, the *Rubaiyyat,* was more renowned in Islamic history as an astronomer. He was head of the observatory in the Persian city of Rayy and produced a solar calendar far more accurate than its Gregorian counterpart used in the Christian West.

Astronomy was also useful to traders. Samarkand was at the center of the "silk route" that linked the Eastern Mediterranean with China, a land which the Muslims had partly conquered in the early 8th century. Between then and the 16th century, the Indian Ocean was exclusively a Muslim basin.

Combination of Chinese and Arabic calligraphy.

There is no tension in Islạm between devotion and business affairs:

"O you who believe! Squander not your wealth among yourselves in vanity, except it be a trade by mutual consent."

Koran 4:29

Many pilgrims to Mecca sustained themselves by trade and relied in their travels on the detailed maps of the world produced by Muslims.

These maps helped the Muslims determine their location with respect to Mecca for prayer and pilgrimage, identify place-names mentioned in the Koran and in the *Hadith* and locate religious sites associated with the Prophet ◗ and the first four Caliphs.

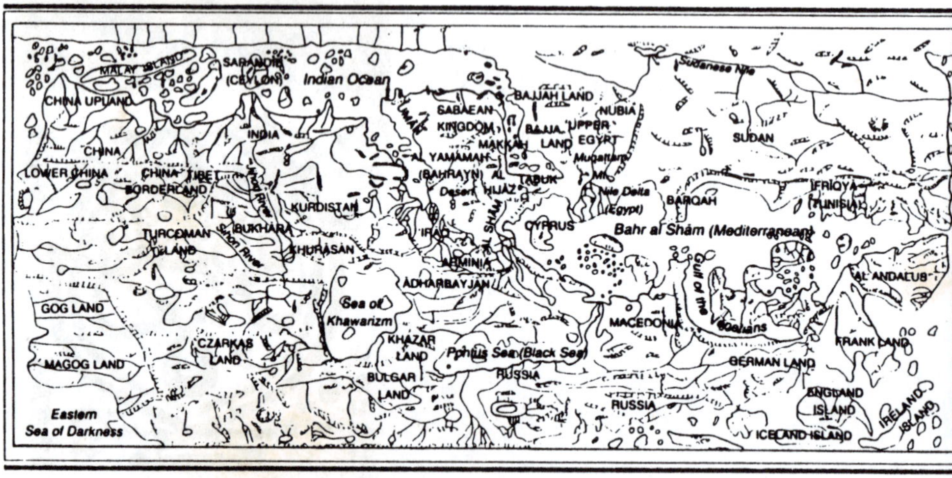

Al-Idrisi's map - translated into English.
In keeping with Muslim geographic tradition, the map places the South at the top of the page.

✸ AL-IDRISI ✸

(1100-1166)

studied in Cordova and lived in Palermo, Sicily, where he prepared for King Roger II The Book of Roger with an Atlas (from the Arabic word for "smooth") of the world, based on collected empirical data.

To the Far East and to the European West, Muslim traders carried silks and textiles. That is why many

✱ TEXTILES ✱

derive their names from Arabic and Persian.

Textile products were used extensively by Muslims: until today, the carpet remains the principal furnishing in the mosque. As for the traditional Islamic house, where loose furniture is practically nonexistent, one finds an abundance of carpets, mattresses and cushions. The designs of textile products also influenced tile and mosaic patterns found in Islamic architecture.

To Muslims, there is no separation between religious art and secular craft.

Cairo

Throughout its development, Islam was an urban civilization. Indeed, many verses in the Koran draw on city life for their imagery.

A fine example of the Islamic city is

❖

CAIRO

Al-Qahira
(the victorious)
capital of Egypt.

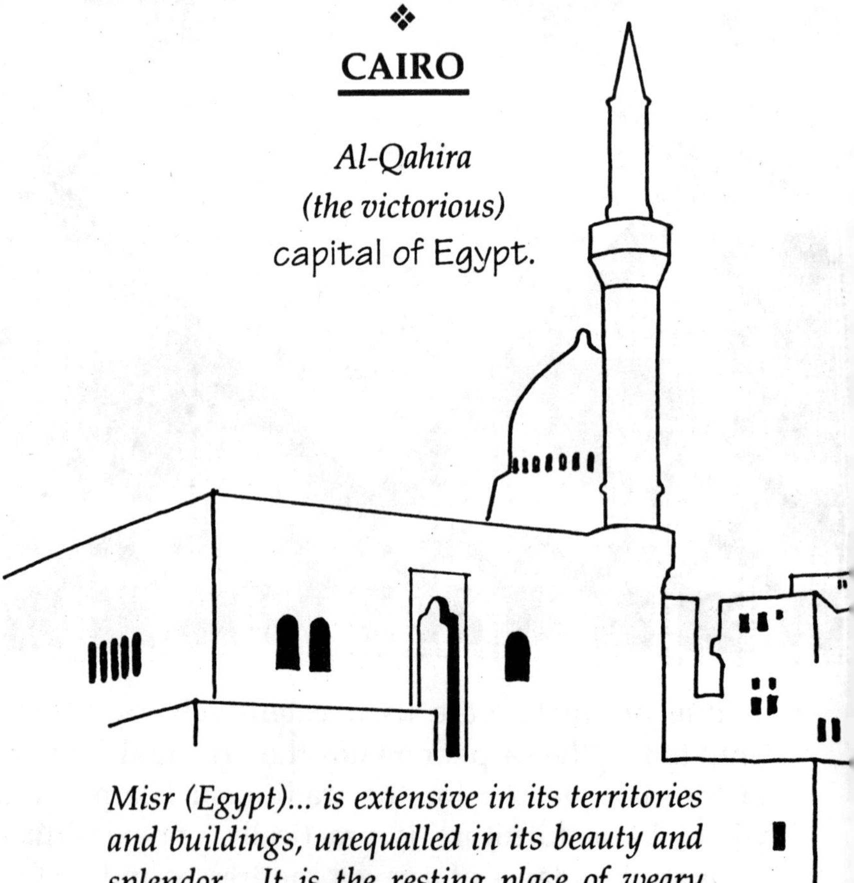

Misr (Egypt)... is extensive in its territories and buildings, unequalled in its beauty and splendor. It is the resting place of weary travellers and the marketplace of rich and poor alike.

Ibn Battuta, 13th-century traveller.

Cairo is among the best preserved of Islamic cities. Follow the traveller through the Gate of Conquests.

The spine of the Islamic city was the

❖ MARKETPLACE ❖

souq

(bazaar in Persian).

Within the market were the baths, street fountains, schools, khans, houses, and mosques. The market is subdivided into separate units specializing in different commodities and crafts.

The *souq* comes alive each day with the smells of spices, the colors of fruits and the sounds of the coppersmiths' pounding.

❖

The
❖ PUBLIC BATH ❖
hammam

was an institution inherited from the Romans. The Muslims, however, did not use it for social interaction and pleasure; the bath was strictly for washing and purification: *"cleanliness is a sign of faith".* Traditionally, separate *hammams* were provided for men and women, with the poorer communities sharing the same facility at different times.

❖ The distinctive sound inside the bath is the clatter of the *Qubqab* (wooden slippers which protect from the heated floor). After changing, bathers relax in the steam room, stretch out for a vigorous rub-down, then proceed to a medium-temperature room to cool down before entering the cold room to splash in water. They then enjoy a cup of tea or coffee as the sunlight filters through the pierced dome above.

If your skin is soft, lufa no. 1 is used; if your skin is hard, the choice is the rougher lufa no. 3. You are then so scrubbed even *"your wife won't recognize you when you leave."* ❖

With the long days spent in the marketplace came the need for

❖ STREET FOUNTAINS ❖
sabeel

These fountains, socially useful and artistically appealing, were generally endowed by benefactors. The Koran encouraged charity:

"Do good; for God loves those who do good."
Koran 39:9

An inscription on the fountain would bear a Koranic verse, the date of construction, and the name of the benefactor. The latter would pay for the water to be brought from the Nile and hire an employee to regulate the taps at specific times.

Near many of these fountains, *madrasas* (schools) were endowed for the instruction of the youth. The sister of Saladin, known as *Sit al-Sham* (Lady of Damascus), founded two schools for religious education located near fountains.

The largest

❖ **MADRASA** ❖
religious school

in Egypt is that of **Sultan Hasan** (1356-1363). It is 85,100 square feet and consists of a school, a mosque, and a mausoleum for the Sultan. The 15th-century historian **al-Maqrizi** considered it an architectural wonder.

This *madrasa* is typical of Islamic architecture in combining the public function (teaching) with the private function (burial). Four large halls *(Iwans)* open onto a central courtyard *(Sahn)*. The *Iwans* are for instruction in each of the **Four Schools of Sunni Islam.** Most schools followed this four-fold division.

Grammar, philosophy and natural sciences were also taught. The Koran had encouraged the pursuit of learning:

> *"Are those who know equal with those who know not?"*
>
> *Koran 2:195*

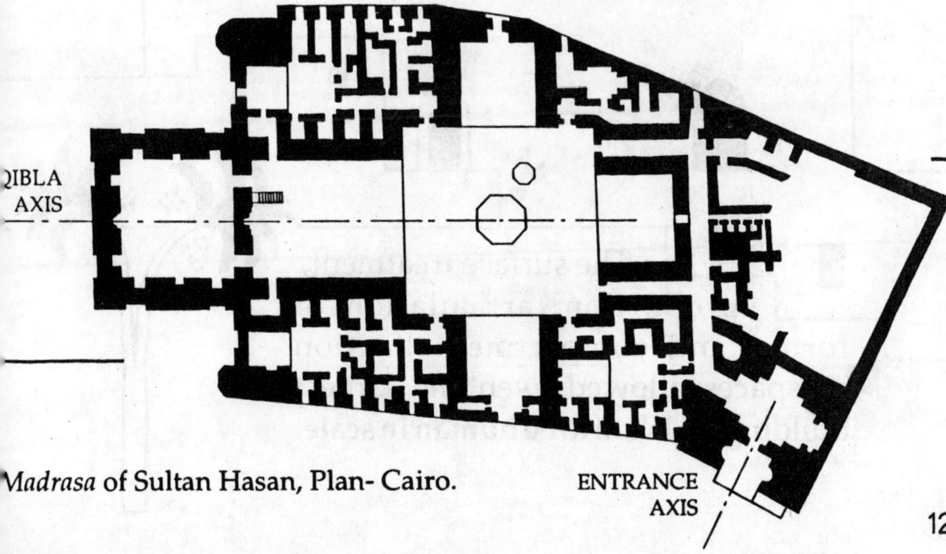

Madrasa of Sultan Hasan, Plan- Cairo.

Visitors to the city stayed in the

❖ KHAN ❖

Inn

a two-storey complex overlooking a central courtyard. The lower storeys provided stables and storage space, while the upper served as apartments.

A famous khan in Cairo was **Khan al-Khaleeli,** the "khan of the man from Hebron", built in the 15th century. Today, the name designates the largest touristic marketplace in Egypt. Many of the novels of Nobel Prize winner Najeeb Mahfouz are set in this area of Cairo where the author still lives.

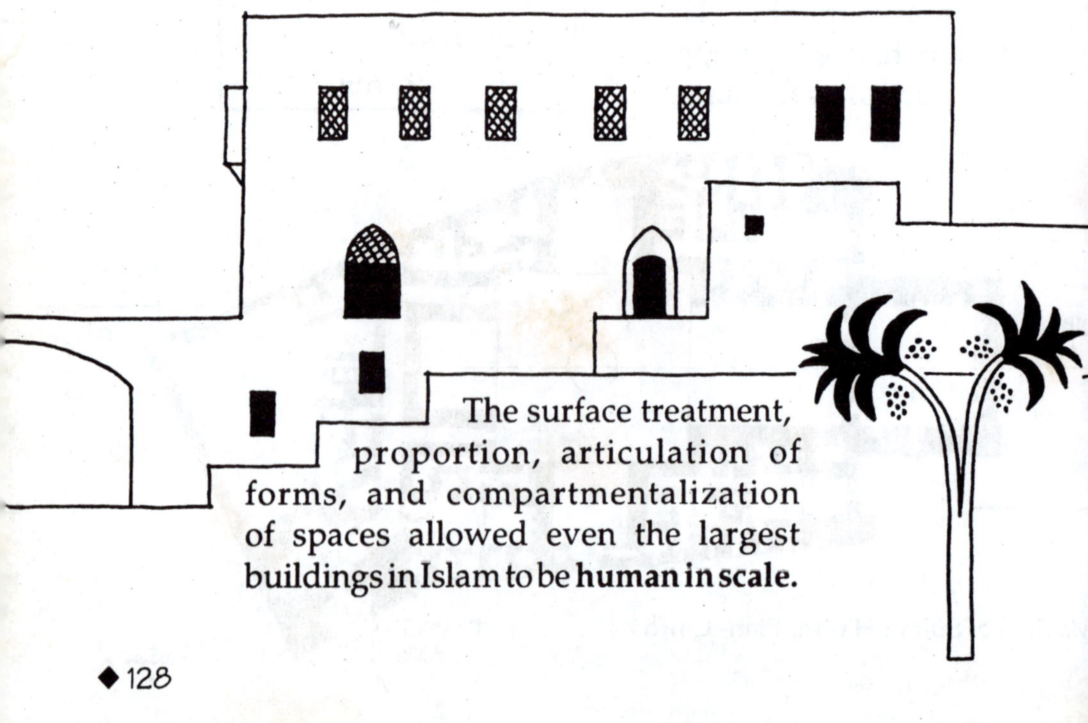

The surface treatment, proportion, articulation of forms, and compartmentalization of spaces allowed even the largest buildings in Islam to be **human in scale.**

. . .

Outside the city was the

❖ CARAVANSERAI ❖

Road Inn

"where travellers alight with their beasts. At each caravanserai is a public watering-place and a shop at which they buy what they need for themselves and their beasts."

The traveller Ibn Battuta on the road from Egypt via Palestine to Syria in 1326.

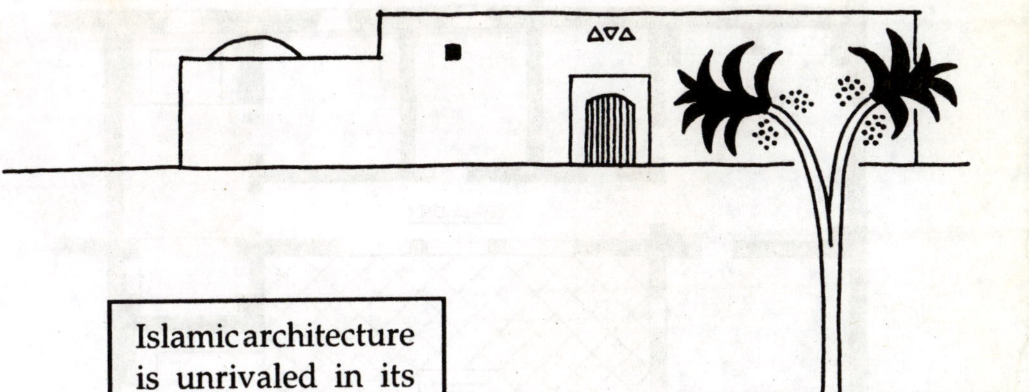

Islamic architecture is unrivaled in its control of **lighting** and **ventilation.**

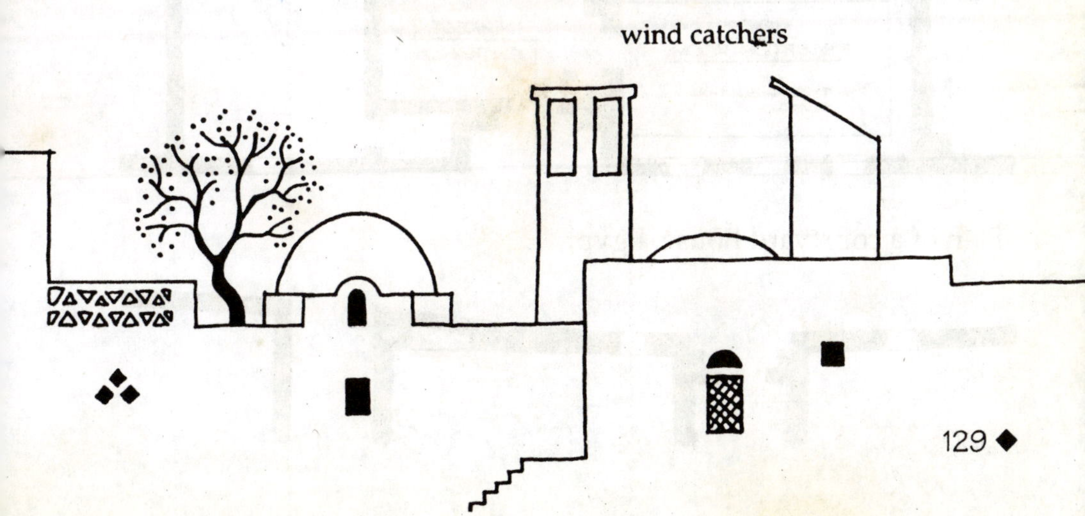

If the traveller had relatives or friends in the city, he would stay in their house.

The

❖ ISLAMIC HOUSE ❖

was inward-looking and consisted of an interior square or rectangular courtyard surrounded by the living quarters. The courtyard provided privacy, ventilated the house, and allowed for outdoor activities away from street dust and heat.

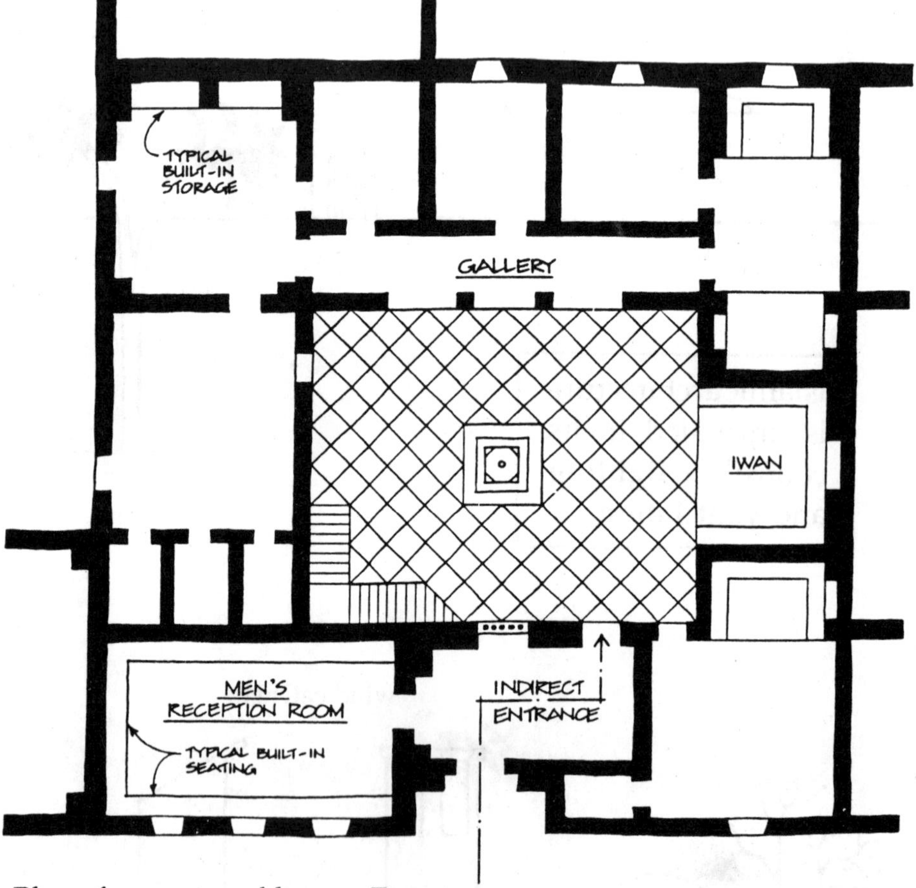

Plan of a courtyard house, Egypt.

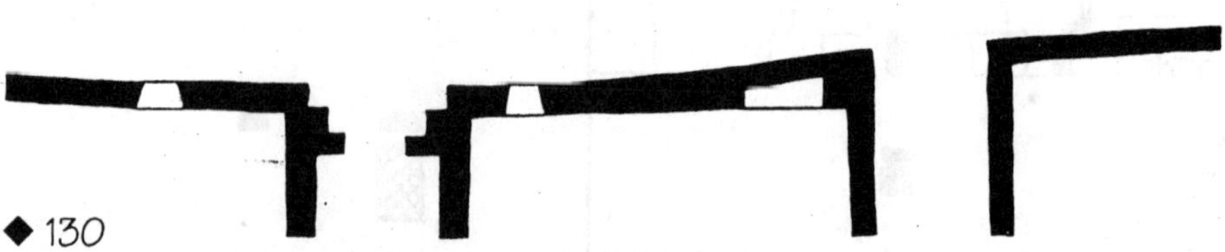

An interesting architectural feature in the Islamic city, seen particularly in housing, is the ***musharabiyya.*** A delicate turned-wood screen, the *musharabiyya* filters sunlight, admits air and permits those inside to look out without being seen.

The **indirect entrance** acts as a visual barrier, sound buffer and psychological break between "out" and "in". In a crowded city, the indirect entrance of the mosque also provides the transition space between the main facade which aligns with the street, and the Qibla axis which dictates the internal orientation (see plan page 127).

The courtyard house is unique in its energy-conserving use of internal climate.

Traditionally, exterior house facades are kept sedate, without any display of wealth. Only after entering the house can the visitor recognize the host's social standing in the community.

Arches, vaults and **domes** are dominant features in Islamic architecture. The variety of styles and building materials reflects the geographical diversity of the Islamic people. It was through Islam that the pointed arch and vault were introduced to Europe.

The focus of the Islamic city was the **Community Mosque.** In Cairo, the oldest community mosque is

❖ **AL-AZHAR** ❖

built in 970, one year after the foundation of the city, and probably named after the Prophet's daughter, Fatima az-Zahra'.

Al-Azhar is one of the greatest institutions for Islamic learning and the oldest continuously functioning university in the western hemisphere. But since Islam has no religious hierarchy, no institution, however prestigious, has authority over the faith of believers.

It was in Mamluke Cairo that the crescent first decorated the cuppola (from Arabic Qubba) of the mosque. Nearly every mosque now has a crescent.

■ In Cairo is buried the father of the sciences of anthropology and economics, the historiographer **Ibn Khaldoon** (1332-1406)

For Ibn Khaldoon, the basic form of civilized society was the city: because man in the city was sophisticated and open-minded, he was less prone to war and ultimately weaker than the Bedouin. With his strong tribal bond (*asabiyya*), the Bedouin successfully invaded and prevailed over the city; but within four generations, he would be corrupted by the city and defeated by a new generation of advancing Bedouins.

Ibn Khaldoon's *Al-Muqaddima* (the Introduction) applied structured reasoning to history and proposed a theory of civilization that is without parallel in ancient or medieval writings.

Djenne

From Cairo, and the neighboring city of Kairawan in Tunisia, Islam spread to North and Central Africa and reached

●

DJENNE

in Mali
whose empire flourished between
the 13th and 16th centuries.

Islam was successful in gaining converts because the preachers and traders who proclaimed it were akin to the African population in culture and skin color, and because the message of Islam affirmed racial equality.

In a *Hadith,* the Prophet ◗ declared:

"People: God is One and your Father is One. Arabs are not superior to non-Arabs, nor are non-Arabs superior to Arabs; nor is the black superior to the red, nor the red to the black - except in piety."

Prophetic Hadith

The eastern facade of the Djenne mosque in Mali points to Mecca. As with other mosques in Africa-- known as the Sudanic mosques-- the governing architectural principle is simplicity. In a *Hadith*, the Prophet ◗ advised:

"I have not been commanded to decorate the mosques."

■ In 1352, the traveller Ibn Battuta visited Mali in Central Africa and wrote about the Muslim inhabitants:

"The black people possess some admirable qualities. They are seldom unjust and have a greater abhorrence of injustice than any other people. There is complete security in their country. Neither traveller nor inhabitant in it has anything to fear from robbers or men of violence. They do not confiscate the property of any white man who dies in their country, even if it be uncounted wealth. They are careful to observe the hours of prayer, and assiduous in attending them in congregations and in bringing up their children to them."

Trans. H.A.R. Gibb.

For hundreds of years, scholars from as far as Baghdad and Cordova travelled to the African mosques to study theology and mysticism.

The capital of the Mali Empire was

● TIMBUCTOO ●

a city that had grown around its mosques.

Timbuctoo boasted extensive private libraries, and served as the center of learning south of the Sahara. From it missionaries travelled to Ghana, the Ivory Coast, Guinea and other locations and established Koran schools that continue today.

The intellectual and the social greatness of Central Africa coincide with the growth of Islam. From the Nile to the Niger, and from the 8th to the 18th century, powerful cultures emerged in Songhai, Kanem-Bornu and Benin that were rooted in the language and imagination of Islam.

Thus Arabic appears in the Hausa and Swahili languages; indeed, the word Swahili derives from the Arabic word for "coast".

In Africa evolved Sufi orders organized around families whose blood bore *barakat* (miraculous blessings). From Nigeria to Morocco, the countryside is dotted with shrines of the Marabouts (holy persons) whose invocation could result in miracles.

Istanbul

At the beginning of the 16th century, all North Africa fell to the new Muslim power of the Ottoman Turks whose capital was

◆

ISTANBUL

once Constantinople
(the name was officially changed in 1930).

From the 14th until the 16th century, the Ottomans had the most powerful army in the world. Even after its decline, it was still remembered for its might and its marching music. Thus Mozart's **"Turkish March".**

By the early 1800's, American musicians adopted Turkish-style instruments like the tenor drum, bass drum, cymbal, and crescent.

A Turkish Janissary.

Both European and American bands of the 18th and 19th centuries included instrumentalists dressed in Janissary costume.

Muslim armies had a central elite corps that was surrounded by a multi-racial soldiery. The famous fighting force of the Ottoman army was the **Janissary** (the "new soldiers"). They were Christian slaves raised from childhood in military discipline, Koranic orthodoxy and celibacy.

It is through them that the **Scimitar** (Sabre) became associated with Islam.

■ The Koran did not prohibit war, but limited its application to particular conditions. War was not to be waged for territorial gain, nor for racial superiority, nor for power.

War was for the establishment of faith and social justice and for the eradication of evil.

A 16th-century woodcut from Germany. Contrast the Turkish horsemen (right) in their light armor and the ponderous Christian cavalry.

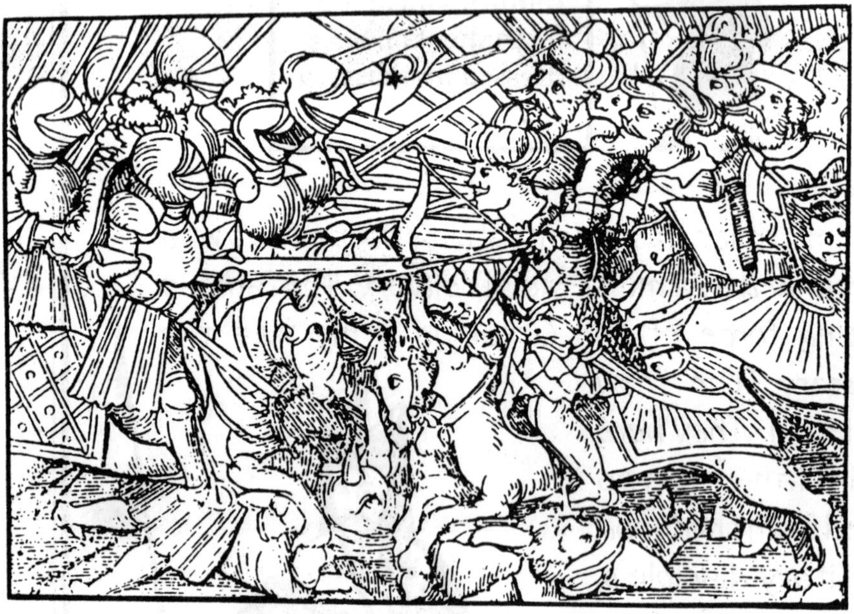

Women and children, the religious and the aged, were not to be harmed. Those who died in battle were to be remembered as martyrs of faith:

"Never think that those who were slain in the cause of God are dead. They are alive, and will be provided for by their Lord."

Koran 3:169

The Janissaries extended Islam into the heart of Europe and reached Vienna, where no Muslim had ever fought.

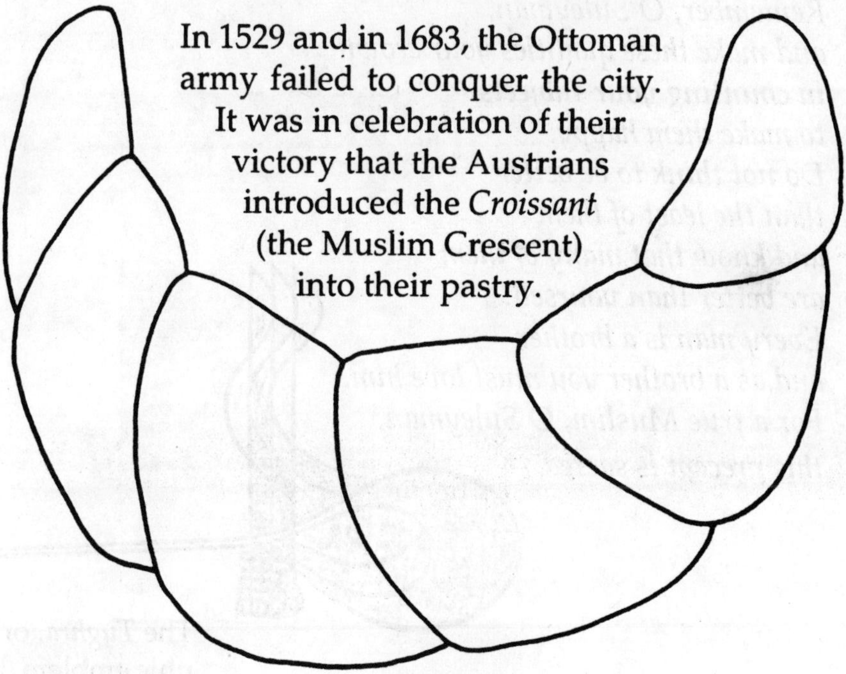

In 1529 and in 1683, the Ottoman army failed to conquer the city. It was in celebration of their victory that the Austrians introduced the *Croissant* (the Muslim Crescent) into their pastry.

The Janissaries reached their height under

◆ SULEYMAN THE LAWMAKER ◆

(fl. 1520-1566)

Roads and caravanserais were built, trades and crafts flourished, and social services were so extended that the Muslim Empire became a welfare state with all the benefits of an efficient bureaucracy and legal system. Thus this poem by Suleyman:

To be charitable and kind
is the glory of the throne.
Remember, O Suleyman,
and make these qualities your crown
in counting your subjects
to make them happy.
Do not think to be better
than the least of them
and know that many of them
are better than yourself.
Every man is a brother
and as a brother you must love him.
For a true Muslim, O Suleyman,
this precept is sacred.

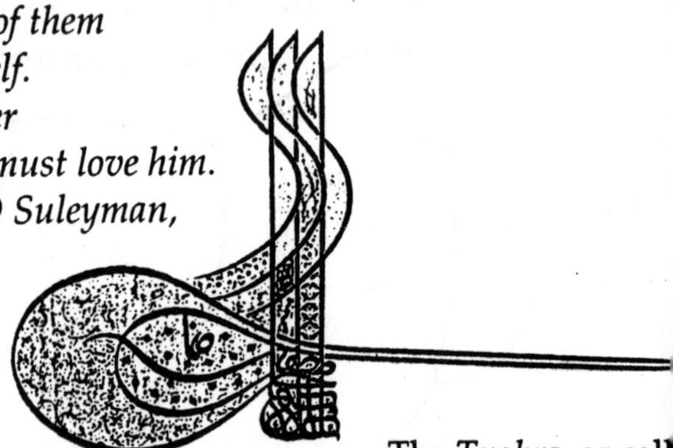

The *Tughra*, or call
phic emblem, bear
Suleyman's name.

In Suleyman, power was not divested from piety.

Under Suleyman, the population grew: after Jews were expelled from Catholic Spain in 1492, they found refuge in the Muslim Empire.

Another reason for growth was the conversion of European and Eastern Christians to Islam.

A Jewish merchant by a 16th-century French traveller.

"Seeing how many daily go from us to them," wrote the English traveller Henry Blount in 1636, *"and how few of theirs to us, it appears of what consequence the prosperity of Islam is to draw men upon it."*

Still, from the beginnings of Islam until today, Christians have remained and prospered in Muslim lands. In contrast, the Christian Reconquest in 15th-century Spain left few Muslims and fewer mosques.

One of the most famous converts to Islam was

◆ **SINAN** ◆
(b. 1491),
the court architect.

Born in Anatolia, he rose through the Janissary system to design 334 buildings for Suleyman and his successor.

In 1560, Sinan completed the **Sulaymaniyya Complex** in Istanbul. It consisted of a mosque surrounded by seven colleges, a hospital and an asylum, a bath, a soup kitchen, schools, fountains, wrestling grounds, shops, and the tomb of Suleyman all covered by 500 domes.

In this mosque, Sinan proved that he could surpass the greatest design in Byzantine architecture- St. Sophia. The Sulaymaniyya was his masterpiece.

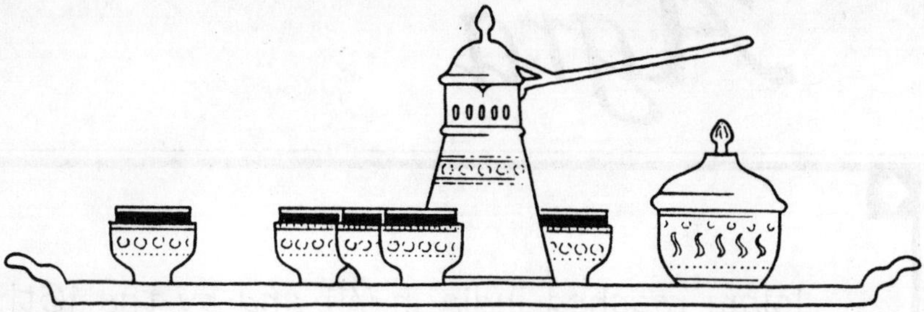

The Ottomans popularized the

◆ COFFEE-HOUSE ◆

The coffee bean had long been used in Yemen, and the first coffee-house originated in Aleppo, Syria. The concept of the coffee-house then spread from Istanbul to Vienna and the rest of the world.

Tulips (from the Persian word for "Turban") were also introduced to Europe during the reign of Suleyman. In the 17th century, England, Holland and France were seized by "Tulipomania", when certain tulip bulbs were worth 250 sheep.

In the 18th century, **Sultan Ahmad III** turned his rule into the Reign of the Tulip. Every April, when the moon was full, the Sultan would organize a Tulip Festival in which turtles with candles on their backs lit up the tulip gardens. The tulip as an artistic motif appears in Islamic art from Istanbul to India.

Agra

Islam reached India in 711 and by the 16th century had culminated in the **Mughal Empire** with

◆

AGRA

as the capital. In 1638, it was moved to Delhi, which remains India's capital.

The height of the Mughal (from the word Mongol) Empire was between 1526 and 1707. The last Mughal emperor was sent into exile by the British in 1858.

The palace administration and court life of the Mughals included poetry readings, musical recitals and **Chess.**
Through the Muslims of India, and from the 8th century on, chess spread to the rest of the world. The language of the Mughal court was Persian, and "Check mate" derives from the Persian words *Shah mat* (the king is dead).

■ Although India was under Islamic rule, Muslims represented only a minority of the population, the prevailing religion being Hinduism. Hindus, with their indigenously vibrant culture, had little interaction with Muslims outside the urban centers of imperial power. To meet this challenge of a minority ruling the majority,

✦ **AKBAR** ✦
(1542-1605)

one of the greatest Muslim kings of India,
instituted toleration.

Akbar reconciled Islam and Hinduism: he introduced a fair system of revenue assessment and appointed a Hindu as his imperial minister. He also removed the extra tax which Islam imposed on Hindus, replaced the lunar with the solar calendar and ordered Muslims not to slaughter cows.

Akbar had sensitive artistic taste. He is accredited with the beginning of **Mughal Painting and Miniature.**

Akbar brought artists from the Safavid court in Isfahan to supervise his studio, known as *Kitab Khaneh.* Over a hundred painters, many of them Hindu, illustrated Arabic, Persian and Indian manuscripts.

Realism marked the work of **Mansur,** "Wonder of the Age", during the reign of Akbar's son, **Jahangir,** who brought Persian mores and manners to court.

The greatest of Indo-Islamic arts was architecture, which prospered under **Shah Jahan, Akbar's grandson**. When his wife **Mumtaz Mahal** died in 1631, he decided to build for her in Agra the supreme garden tomb, the

✦ TAJ MAHAL ✦

Over 22,000 expert craftsmen from India, Asia and Europe were employed for 22 years (1632-1654) in the building of this *"miracle of miracles, the final wonder of the world"*. Various architects worked on the project, including the Emperor himself.

The Taj Mahal fuses both the Muslim and Hindu style. The pointed arch, the onion-shaped dome and the arabesque are Muslim-inspired. The Hindu influence is apparent in the white marble, the perforated grills and the emphasis on geometrical relationships within the building (the overall plan is typical of other Mughal tombs in Delhi and Sikandra).

Southeast Asia

From India, Islam spread to the neighboring islands of Sri Lanka and the Maldives, and then to Southeast Asia. At a time when Christians were colonizing America, Muslims were converting the peoples of Malaysia, Southern Philippines and Indonesia. Indian and Arab teachers preached Islam and peacefully overpowered the strong Hindu-Buddhist culture with the clarity of the Koranic creed; they also revolutionized social organization by freeing the common man from Hindu caste bondage.

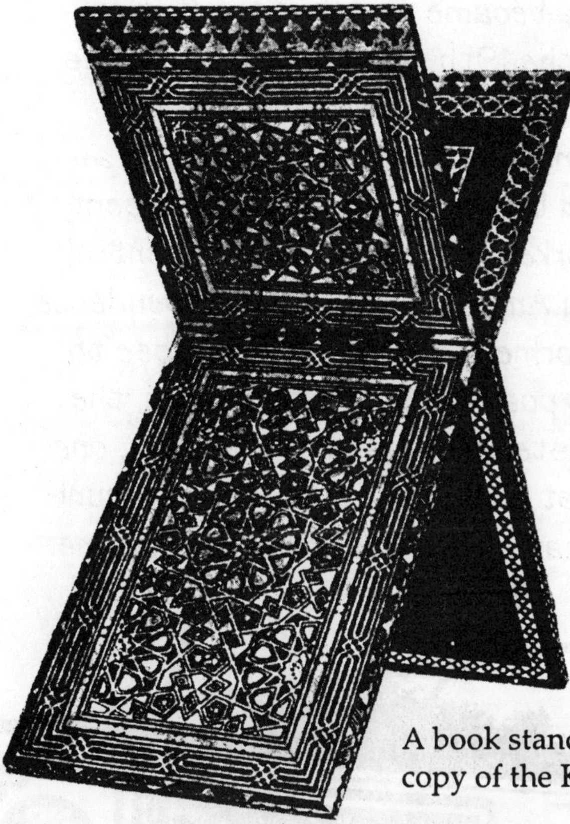

A book stand for a large copy of the Koran.

Indonesia is 90% Muslim and has the world's largest Muslim population (174,900,000) in any one country. Pakistan, which gained independence in 1947 to establish an Islamic state (the word Pakistan means "Land of the Pure"), comes second.

Central and South

After India became a part of the British Empire in the 19th century, many Muslims were sent to the Caribbean Island of Trinidad and to Guyana and Suriname as indentured laborers. The Dutch also sent Muslim workers from Indonesia to Central and South America. With the independence of these former colonies, Muslims rose to prominent positions: Hamilton Green, the prime minister of Guyana, is a Muslim; one of the most successful business communities in Panama consists of Indian Muslims.

America

At the turn of this century, thousands of Muslims emigrated from Lebanon, Syria, Palestine, Persia and other Middle Eastern countries, and settled in South America to work as traders. Some Muslims adapted their names to Spanish as in the case of the president of Argentina, Carlos Menem (whose Syrian parents converted to Christianity from Islam); others strengthened their community faith by building mosques, often in the style of their Arabic or Iranian tradition.

Brazil has the largest Muslim population (half a million) in South America. Argentina comes second (350,000 Muslims), but the small country of Guyana boasts the highest number of mosques- 130 mosques for just under 75,000 worshippers. There are about a million and a half Muslims in South America.

United States

In the United States live nearly four million Muslims consisting of converts and emigrants.

The emigrants came at the end of the 19th century from Arab countries and built the first mosque in North America in Cedar Rapids (1934). They also built the first all-Muslim cemetery in Mecca. In 1953, the soldier's dogtag began to include "I" to refer to the America of Islamic faith; in June 1991, and for the first time, a Muslim Imam gave the invocation at the chamber of Congress.

The Muslims have found welcome in predominantly-Christian America:

"The church and the Muslim community are related by history and by God as an expression and application of the covenant of Abraham. Islam has its place in God's purpose in election and creation."

The Reformed Church of America.

Momentum to Islam in the United States has come from African-Americans who have turned to the Koranic teaching of racial equality with profound conviction. Although the early stirrings of Islam included among them unorthodox elements, there was a return to the doctrines of the Koran and the Sunna under the charismatic leadership of **Malcolm X.**

Cassius Clay, a friend of Malcolm X, converted to Islam and changed his name to Muhammad Ali.

After going to Mecca on pilgrimage, Malcolm X praised the anti-racialism of Islam:

"I remember one night," he wrote, *"I lay awake amid sleeping Muslim brothers and I learned that pilgrims from every land- every color and class and rank, high officials and beggars alike, all snored in the same language."*

Europe

Muslims from India and from other countries of the Commonwealth emigrated to England. Today, Muslims constitute nearly 4% of the population of the United Kingdom. The situation is similar in France, where North African Muslims from the former French colonies of Algiers, Tunisia and Morocco have settled. In Germany, nearly 5% of the population consists of Muslim "Visitor Workers".

The oldest mosque in Germany.

Islam today is the second largest religion in Europe. There are significant Muslim populations of professionals, workers and students in every region of Western Europe.

In their new European homes, Muslims have cherished their religious traditions, along with their distinctive cultural and moral heritage. Whether in Holland or in Spain, they turn to Mecca during prayer, give their children Koranic names and study Arabic to master theology.

European religious and secular institutions have cooperated with the immigrants: in 1973, the Vatican city donated land for the construction of a mosque to serve Italy's one million Muslims, and a year later, Belgium recognized Islamic Law as the legal code of its Muslim community.

In 1966, the Documents of Vatican II declared:

"Upon the Muslims, too, the church looks with esteem. They adore one God, living and enduring, merciful and all-powerful, Maker of heaven and earth ***and*** *Speaker to men... They prize the* ***moral life, and*** *give worship to God especially* ***through prayer,*** *almsgiving* ***and*** *fasting."*

■ In their attempts to sustain their religious identity, however, Muslims have posed difficult challenges to the European social and legal system: should the Muslim teacher at state-run schools be allowed time for the five daily prayers? Should the sexes be separated in the classroom? Should girls be allowed their head cover at secular schools? Should the ritual slaughter of animals at the *Adha* feast be permitted without government inspection?

A Muslim in The Hague, Holland.

The differences which Muslims exhibit have led to violent outbursts against them. Unemployed laborers, Neo-Nazis and xenophobes have mistakenly linked the immigrants to social and industrial failure.

Attacks on Immigrants Raising Concern in Italy

LA VIOLENCE

Nazi-inspired thuggery seems to be surfacing in Italy as in much of Europe.

In chaotic regional elections, voters reject the entire Establishment and give new power to anti-foreign, anti-immigrant nationalists

The victory of the extreme right-wing party in the recent French elections is proof of the rising tide of hatred and intolerance against Muslims in Europe.

■ These are the countries in the world which have a Muslim majority or near-majority (above 50%).

Afghanistan (Central Asia)
Albania (Europe)
Algeria (Mediterranean Basin)
Brunei (Southeast Asia)
Chad (Central Africa)
Djibouti (East Africa)
Egypt (Mediterranean Basin)
Gabon (West Africa)
Gambia (West Africa)
Guinea (West Africa)
Gunae-Bissau (West Africa)
Indonesia (Southeast Asia)
Iran (Central Asia)
Iraq (West Asia)
Jordan (West Asia)
Kuwait (Persian Gulf)
Lebanon (Mediterranean Basin)
Libya (Mediterranean Basin)
Malaysia (Southeast Asia)
Maldives (Indian Ocean)

Mali (West Africa)
Mauritania (Northwest Africa)
Morocco (Mediterranean Basin)
Niger (North-Central Asia)
Nigeria (West Africa)
Oman (Persian Gulf)
Pakistan (South Asia)
Palestine (Mediterranean Basin)
Qatar (Persian Gulf)
Saudi Arabia (Southwest Asia)
Senegal (West Africa)
Sierra Leone (West Africa)
Somalia (East Africa)
Sudan (East Africa)
Syria (Mediterranean Basin)
Tunisia (Mediterranean Basin)
Turkey (Mediterranean Basin)
United Arab Emirates (Persian Gulf)
Yemen (Red Sea)

In the former Soviet Union, Kazakhstan, Uzbekistan, Azerbaijan, Turkmenistan, Tajikistan and Kyrgyzstan all have Muslim majorities.

Regardless of nationality or color, race or social status, sex or language, Muslims view themselves as one community in submission to God.

And regardless of historic, geographic or cultural differences, Muslims share the light of God in the Koran.

"God is the light of the heavens and the earth. His light may be compared to a niche that enshrines a lamp, the lamp within a crystal star-like brilliance. It is lit from a blessed olive tree neither eastern or western. Its very oil would almost shine forth, though no fire touched it. Light upon light; God guides to His light whom He will."

Koran 24:35

STRAIGHT PATH

"So let there be a body among you who may call to the good, enjoin what is esteemed and forbid what is odious. They are those who will be successful."

Koran 3:104

By the end of World War I in 1918, nearly all the lands of Islam were ruled by

Britain, France, Holland, Russia, and Italy.

Capitals like Damascus and Baghdad which had never been conquered came under Western colonization, and in 1917, British forces led by General Allenby entered Jerusalem. Indicative of Britain's dismissive attitude towards the inhabitants of Palestine, the Proclamation was published in English, French and Italian, but not in the native language of the people, Arabic.

PROCLAMATION

OF MARTIAL LAW IN JERUSALEM.

To the inhabitants of Jerusalem the Blessed and the people dwelling in its vicinity.

The defeat inflicted upon the Turks by the troops under my command has resulted in the occupation of your City by my forces. I therefore here and now proclaim it to be under Martial Law, under which form of administration it will remain so long as military considerations make it necessary.

However, lest any of you should be alarmed by reason of your experiences at the hands of the enemy who has retired, I hereby inform you that it is my desire that every person should pursue his lawful business without fear of interruption. Furthermore, since your City is regarded with affection by the adherents of three of the great religions of mankind, and its soil has been consecrated by the prayers and pilgrimages of devout people of those three religions for many centuries, therefore do I make known to you that every sacred building, monument, holy spot, shrine, traditional site, endowment, pious bequest or customary place of prayer, of whatsoever form of the three religions, will be maintained and protected according to the existing customs and beliefs of those to whose faiths they are sacred.

December 1917.

EDMUND HENRY HYNMAN ALLENBY, General,

Commander-in-Chief Egyptian Expeditionary Force.

The only Muslim capital that was spared was Istanbul.

The Western countries exploited the natural resources of *Dar-al-Islam*, "Abode of Islam," and turned it into a market for their exports. In so doing, they divided the Muslim Umma into...

n
of
ely
ural
erely
per.

NATION STATES

The defeat of the Ottomans-- the last Muslim Empire-- had left the Umma without a political center. While the European territory of the Empire was absorbed by the Soviet Union, the African and Asiatic territories were partitioned into states by England and France, the European powers most active in colonization.

This partitioning was an arbitrary act: the borders of the new states rarely reflected natural or cultural identity; they were merely slashes of pen on paper.

ning was an
ct: the borders
ew states rarely
natural or cultural
y; they were merely
es of pen on paper.

This partitioning was an arbitrary act: the borders of the new states rarely reflected natural or cultural identity; they were merel[y]
slashes of pen on

On the newly emergent nation state, the Western powers installed a ruler who was protective of their interests, and who was culturally and linguistically Westernized. The ruler governed without a system of checks or balances and relied for his protection on a Western - trained internal security system.

He and the ruling elite lived affluently while the majority of the population remained poor, fearful and disenfranchised. The West which had installed him urged neither social nor political change: what was good in a Western democracy was to be denied the Muslim subjects.

The Shah of Iran.

Since the creation of the independent states, Muslims have tried to identify the path towards political stability, modernization and religious continuity.

◆

FOUR MODELS
have been tried:

ا

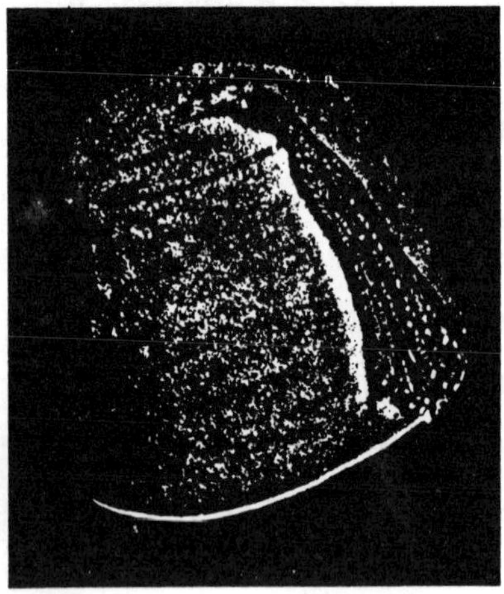

The model of secularization was adopted chiefly by **Turkey.** Under its leader Mustapha Kamal (Attaturk), the Turks changed their script from the Arabic to the Roman alphabet, abolished the caliphate, replaced Koranic law with a legal system derived from France, and discarded the Ottoman head gear (the fez) in favor of the hat.

A

In the 1930's and under Reza Shah, **Iran** also downplayed its Islamic character in favor of its pre-Islamic Sassanian roots; in **Indonesia,** the state formulated a universalistic ideology, *Pancasila,* "the five principles", which governed all social, political and educational institutions.

Secularization exclusively affected the urban centers and the ruling socio-economic groups: it did not touch the lives of the majority of the people who viewed it as an imposition from the West (Iran) or the Communist East (Indonesia).

As a result, the peoples reacted: in 1978, Iran became an Islamic Republic.

Ayatullah Khomeini was influenced by the Pakistani theologian **Mawlana Mawdudi** (1903-79) who argued for a state applying *Shari'a* and ruled by one man assisted by qualified Koranic interpreters.

Ayatollah Khomeini.

By circulating his sermons on cassette, Khomeini could reach the disaffected both inside Iran and elsewhere among Muslims. From Nigeria to Malaysia, Khomeini became the hero who would overturn secularism and defeat the West, "the great Satan".

From the 18th century on, some Muslim theologians emphasized the harmony between Islam and the modern society of the West. Once the Koran was interpreted in its rational meaning, they argued, there would be no apparent difference between its vision of human life under God and the challenges of technological and industrial society.

For instance,

- **Democracy** is equivalent to the Koranic principle of *Shura* (consultation of the ruler with others), which King Fahd applied in Saudi Arabia in 1992;
- **Public opinion** is consensus of the community;
- **Abortion** is not allowed except in cases of danger to the mother on the basis of the Koran's prohibition of murder;
- Attention to the **environment** is identified with God's role as creator and preserver of heaven and earth, and with man's duty to respect God's workmanship;
- **Science** is encouraged because the Koran, more than any other monotheistic text, advocates research and inquiry.

The founder of this harmonizing trend in Islam is the theologian from Central Asia, **Jamal al-Din al-Afghani** (1839-97) and his disciple **Mohammad Abdu.** Both taught at al-Azhar mosque in Cairo, and their teachings touched the whole world of Islam.

Mohammad Abdu.

From Indonesia to Malaysia, and from Jordan, Syria, Morocco, to Mauritania and Nigeria (the largest Muslim state in Africa), the impact of this harmony has continued to the present:

Subjects live under a **constitution** derived from the West that governs the state's international affairs, banking system and trading agreements; and under ***shari'a*** law that governs marriage, divorce, inheritance, punishment and other personal matters.

In civil affairs, Non-Muslim subjects of a Muslim state follow the laws of their religious community.

III. The Model of SOCIALISM

Recognizing that the Koran preaches social equality, revolutions were launched to remove rulers who had used capitalism and free market economy to invite foreign investments. The famous proponent of socialism was the Egyptian leader **Jamal abdul Nasser** (1911-1970). His socialism resulted in the nationalization of foreign companies, the appropriation of land from feudal landlords and its redistribution among Egyptian peasants. Although Nasser presented socialism in secular terms, he still relied on religious justification:

for him **"Islam is revolution.**

Nasser was so admired that upon his death over half a dozen people committed suicide in grief.

With the demise of Communism, the appeal of the socialist model has been largely diminished.

But like secularization and modernization, socialism has not addressed the chief challenge to Islamic society:

how to cope with the impact of the technological and industrial West whose exports to Muslim countries permeate all aspects of life: from food and bottled water, to medicines, weapons, clothes, cars, and entertainment.

Can there be an authentic Islamic society when Muslim daily needs are provided by non-Muslim producers?

In the last quarter of the 20th century, the answer to the above challenge has increasingly drawn on...

IV. The Model of the KORANIC STATE of MEDINA, 623-632 C.E.

The Medinan followers reject the secular consequences of nationalism and want Islamic law to guide the state. They seek to apply Koranic rules to women's dress: women should always cover their heads, arms and legs; to sex segregation: women should be separated from men at school, at work and in transport; to educational curricula: emphasis should be placed on the study of science and theology and on the correlation between modern discoveries and Koranic revelation; to punishments: flogging, amputation and decapitation; and to economic policy.

Thus
ISLAMIC BANKING.

The Koran prohibited usury ("*riba*" 2:275). An alternative form of investment was proposed in Islamic society where no prior interest rate was to be fixed, but where the lender shared in the profit of an enterprise after its completion.

An advertisement in Arabic from the Islamic Bank in Amman, Jordan, stating that: "*Halal* (*Shari'a*-approved) investment is what the Islamic Bank seeks."

The Islamic bank is an international financial organization consisting of governments that are part of **the Organization of the Islamic Conference.** Since initiating its first major project in 1975, the Bank has established branches in over 30 Islamic countries.

The Kingdom of Saudi Arabia, along with the neighboring trucial states, has pursued the goal of government by Koranic law.

The flag of the Kingdom with the *Shahada*
"There is no deity but God,
and Muhammad is His Prophet".
The state is God's.

In 1947, Pakistan became a state for Muslims with a constitution that confirmed:

"Steps shall be taken to enable the Muslims of Pakistan individually and collectively to order their lives in accordance with the Holy Koran and the Shari'a."

In Malaysia, consciousness of an Islamic identity grew into political opposition among the native Malayan.

The argument for the Koranic state depends on precedence. Since alcohol cannot be legally purchased in a Muslim state because of Koranic law, why should the other Koranic codes not be followed?

One of the leading intellectuals advocating the traditionalist model is the Sudanese legal scholar and philosopher, Dr. Hasan Turabi.

In his view, *"Islam is the only force that can fill the vacuum left by the failures of Western-inspired socialism and nationalism. It alone can inspire the young and give them a vision, a sense of allegiance."*

In Jordan and in Algeria, in Azerbaijan and in Kashmir, millions aspire to fill the vacuum by bringing the political and social order under the laws of the Koran. In 1983, Turabi introduced *shari'a* law to Sudan; in 1984, traditionalists prevailed in parts of Lebanon; in 1991, they won the elections in Algeria. In 1992, ? ? ?

In the past two decades, the Islamic simplicity and equality has attracted Muslims in countries where:

- a non-Islamic ideology was used by a nationalist government to unify the people;
- rapid urbanization resulted in polarizing the rich and the poor;
- a ruling class was supported by non-Islamic superpowers;
- rapid economic growth brought the overwhelming technology of the West.

These factors have given rise to a small number of militant Muslims who can cope with this imported culture of high technology only by fighting it.

Hostile to the West for its colonial past, these militants oppose the process of civilization associated with Westernization.

In so doing they seem to ignore the vast intellectual and cultural traditions of Islamic history, and to view Islam as consisting solely of political and legal precepts. For them, faith is law, and law is ideology.

Because the Prophet ◗ kept a beard, so will they; because the Prophet ◗ did not dress in trousers but in a *abaya*, so will they.

The logo of a militant group in Egypt.

Opposition to the West and to Westernization offers a sense of historical identity and the promise of economic autonomy.

More significant in number and impact than the militants are the revivalist movements among Muslims in India, Bangladesh and elsewhere that focus more on community spirituality than on politics. In Nigeria, **the University of Nasr al-Islam** was founded in 1961 to foster religious education; earlier in 1950, **the Society of Usbat ul-Deen** was founded to instruct Nigerian Muslim women. South of Khartoum in Sudan, there is a *Khilwa* (a separate community) that pursues the study of the Koran while cultivating the land.

In 1980, which coincided with the beginning of the 15th Hijra century, the first Islamic village in the United States was designed by the Egyptian architect, Hassan Fathy. Located in Abiquiu, New Mexico, the village serves the religious and educational needs of over 30 families.

Numerous Muslim organizations meet regularly to examine the challenges facing the community. They offer help to the poor and the displaced, send teachers to convert non-Muslims and finance medical and social facilities. Neither national, linguistic, ethnic nor social barriers affect their goals.

A 1992 advertisement asking for donations to support Muslim missionaries.

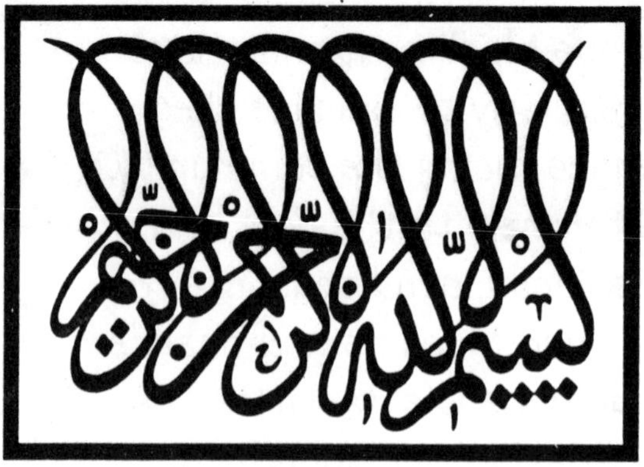

Since the 19th-century beginnings of Western colonization, Muslims have fought to defend their faith and land. The Koran urges spiritual and physical

RESISTANCE

to tyranny.

Imams and Sufis, men and women have defied oppression with their lives and prayers. In the 1980's and 1990's, Islam has continued to rally the community against occupation. Whenever the cause of the Koran is declared, Muslims from all nationalities respond.

> *"Drive them out from the places from which they drove you."*
>
> *Koran 2:191*

...the Mujahideen fought successfully against Communist occupation in **Afghanistan...**

...the Muslim minority has struggled for equal rights in the **Philippines** and in **Bulgaria...**

...Muslims in **Kashmir** are striving for independence...

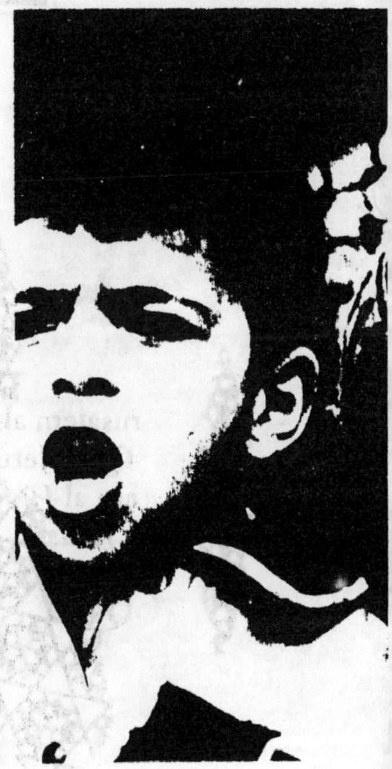

...although **Kuwait** turned to the world community for help against the Iraqi occupation, its internal resistance rallied under the call of Islam...

...Islamic Resistance groups are fighting against Israeli occupation in **South Lebanon...**

...some leaders in the *intifada* have sought Koranic guidance in the struggle to establish the state of **Palestine,** with Jerusalem as capital...

The Dome of the Rock in Jerusalem was built between 688-692 C.E. Jerusalem has been the target of non-Muslims since the Crusaders captured the city in the 11th century C.E. The Crusaders were later expelled.

In 1967,
Jerusalem was again captured
by non-Muslims.

◆

"So do not lose heart or be grieved,
for you will surely prevail
if you are believers."

Koran 3:139

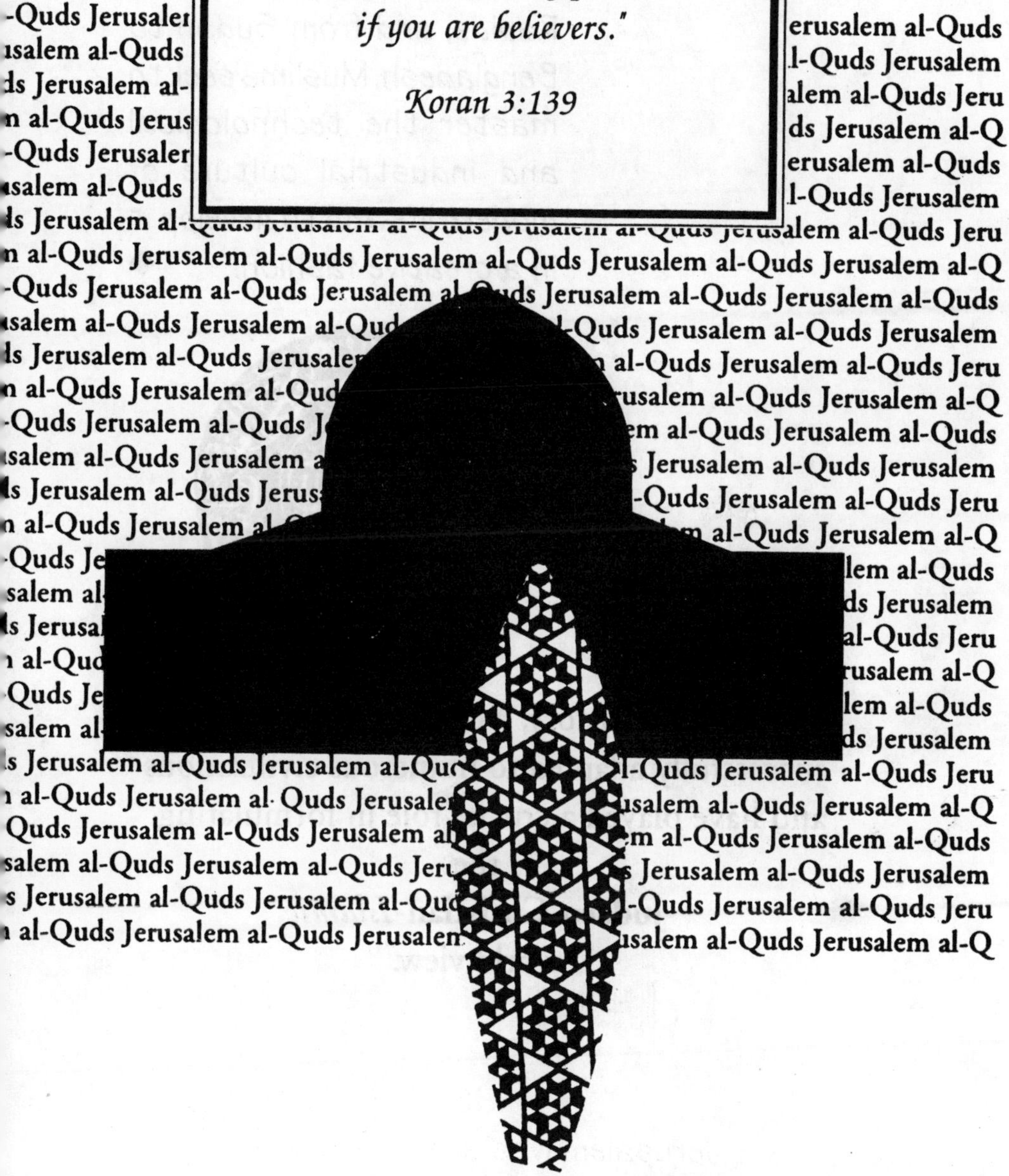

◆ From Jerusalem to Cedar Rapids, and from Sudan to Bengladesh, Muslims seek to master the technological and industrial culture of modern life and to develop it in a creative fashion. ◆

Throughout history, Muslim men and women successfully adapted to numerous civilizations and have played a crucial role in formulating

the

Judaeo-Christian-*Islamic*

world view.

Today,
the challenge facing
Muslims is to expand
this adaptability towards
Westernization without
departing from the
Straight Path
of the **Koran**
and the **Sunna.**

◆

"Guide us in the straight path,
the path of those whom
Thou hast blessed,
not of those against whom
Thou art wrathful,
Nor of those who are astray."

Koran 1: 5-7

Select Bibliography of Books in English

◆ REVELATION

Haykal, Muhammad Husayn *The Life of Mohammad* (n.p. 1976)

Watt, W. Montgomery *Muhammad at Medina* (Oxford, 1981)
---------, *Muhammad at Mecca* (Oxford, 1953)

Burton, John *The Collection of the Qur'an* (Cambridge, 1977)

Juynboll, G.H.A. *Muslim Tradition, Studies in the Chronology, Provenance and Authorship of Early Hadith* (Cambridge, 1983)

Stewart, Desmond *Mecca* (New York, 1980)

Gabrieli, Francesco *Muhammad and the Conquests of Islam,* trans. Virginia Luling and Rosamund Linell (New York, 1968)

Tritton, A.S. *The Caliphs and their Non-Muslim Subjects* (London, 1970)

Endress, Gerhard *An Introduction to Islam,* trans. Carole Hillenbrand (New York, 1988)

◆ COMMUNITY

Michell, George, ed. *Architecture of the Islamic World* (London, 1978 / rep. 1987)

Burckhardt, Titus *Art of Islam* (World of Islam Festival, 1976)

Nelson, Kristina *The Art of Reciting the Qur'an* (Austin, Texas, 1985)

Lings, Martin *The Quranic Art of Calligraphy and Illumination* (World of Islam Festival Trust, 1976)

Walther, Wiebke *Woman in Islam,* trans. C.S.V. Salt (London, 1981)

O'Leary, De Lacy *How Greek Science Passed to the Arabs* (London, 1949)

Khalidi, Tarif *Classical Arab Islam: The Culture and Heritage of the Golden Age* (Princeton, N.J., 1985)

The Genius of Arab Civilization (Cambridge, MA, 1983)

Ullmann, Manfred *Islamic Medicine* (Edinburgh, 1978)

Watt, W. Montgomery *A History of Islamic Spain* (Edinburgh, 1965)

Wade, David *Pattern in Islamic Art* (New York, 1976)

Arberry, A.J. *Sufism: An Account of the Mystics of Islam* (London, 1950)

---------, *Introduction to the History of Sufism* (London, 1943)

Ibn Al-Arabi, Muhyiddin *The Turjuman Al-Ashwaq,* trans. Reynold A. Nicholson (London, 1978)

Blunt, Wilfrid *Isfahan* (London, 1966)

Abu-Lughod, Janet L. *Cairo: 1001 Years of the City Victorious* (Princeton, N.J., 1971)

Ibn Khaldoon *The Muqaddimah,* trans. Franz Rosenthal, ed. N.J. Dawood (Princeton, N.J., 1969)

Clarke, Peter B. *West Africa and Islam* (London, 1982)

Thubron, Colin *Istanbul* (Amsterdam, 1978)

Lord Kinross *The Ottoman Centuries* (New York, 1977)

Penzer, N.M. *The Harem* (London, 1966)

Coles, Paul *The Ottoman Impact on Europe* (London, 1968)

Ahmad, Aziz *Studies in Islamic Culture in the Indian Environment* (Oxford, 1969)

Gascoigne, Bamber *The Great Moghuls* (London, 1971)

Esposito, John L., ed. *Islam in Asia* (New York and Oxford, 1987)

Marsh, Clifton E. *From Black Muslims to Muslims* (Metuchen, N.J., 1984)

Haddad, Yvonne Yazbeck *The Muslims of America* (New York and Oxford, 1991)

◆ STRAIGHT PATH

Zakaria, Rafiq *The Struggle Within Islam* (London, 1988)

Kimmens, Andrew C. *Islamic Politics and the Modern World* (New York, 1991)

Rodinson, Maxime *Islam and Capitalism,* trans. Brian Pearce (Austin, Texas, 1986)

Tibi, Bassam *The Crisis of Modern Islam,* trans. Judith von Sivers (Salt Lake City, 1988)

Said, Edward *Covering Islam* (New York, 1981)

Asali, K.J. *Jerusalem in History* (New York, 1990)

◆ GENERAL

Hitti, Philip K. *Islam and the West: A Historical and Cultural Survey* (London, 1962)

Watt, W. Montgomery *The Majesty that was Islam* (London and New York, 1974)

Islam and the Arab World, ed. Bernard Lewis (New York, 1976)

Robinson, Francis *Atlas of the Islamic World* (New York, 1984)

Acknowledgements and Sources

◆ REVELATION

p. 14 Paccard, Andre *Traditional Islamic Craft in Moroccan Architecture 1* (France, 1980) p. 244

p. 35 Loges, Werner *Turkoman Tribal Rugs* (London, 1980) p. 88

p. 36 Illustration of muezzin inspired by 19th-century lithograph.

p. 46 Farouqui, I. and L. *The Cultural Atlas of Islam* (Macmillan, 1986) p. 39

p. 51 Paccard, Andre *Traditional Islamic Craft in Moroccan Architecture 1* (France, 1980) p. 315

◆ COMMUNITY

p. 72 Hitti, Philip K. *The Origin of the Islamic State* (New York: Columbia Univ., 1916) pp. 186-187

p. 73 "A Special Luster" *Aramco World Magazine* (Sept.-Oct. 1981) pp. 2-3

p. 80 Nelson, Kristina *The Art of Reciting the Qur'an* (Austin: University of Texas Press, 1985) p. 129

p. 88 Burge, T.K. *The Bektashi Order of Dervishes* (London, 1952)

p. 96 Writing Box: "Scheherezade in Paris" *Aramco World Magazine* (Sept.- Oct. 1985) p. 26

p. 97 Illustration inspired by 13th-century miniature.

p. 100 "Deriving Pleasure from Algebra and Alchemy" *Ahlan Wasahlan - Saudi Arabian Airlines* (October 1983) Vol.7, Issue 7, p. 38

p. 103 Ullmann, Manfred *Islamic Medicine* (Edinburgh, 1978) p. 19

p. 107 Scala Museum, Florence, Italy.

p. 109 Paccard, Andre *Traditional Islamic Craft in Moroccan Architecture 1* (France, 1980) p. 257

p. 110 Arberry, A.J. *Sufism* (London, 1950) p. 117

p. 111 Brass Lamp: "Scheherezade in Paris" *Aramco World Magazine* (Sept.- Oct. 1985) p. 30

p. 112 *Persian Miniatures, XIV-XVII Centuries* (Moscow, 1968)

p. 113 *Persian Miniatures, XIV-XVII Centuries* (Moscow, 1968)

p. 115 Clock: "Topkapi's Turkish Timepieces" *Aramco World Magazine* (July- Aug. 1977) p. 10

p. 116 *Aramco World Magazine* (July- Aug. 1977) Rear Cover. The word "Allah" repeated eight times makes up this calligraphic star.

p. 118 *Arab Bank Calendar* (1983) Roland Michaud, Rapho, Paris

p. 119 "Muslims in China- The History" *Aramco World Magazine* (July- Aug. 1985) p. 14

p. 120 Farouqui, I. and L. *The Cultural Atlas of Islam* (Macmillan, 1986) map 25

p. 132 "Calligraphy: The Art of Islam- In the Name of God" *Aramco World Magazine* (July- Aug. 1977) p. 26

p. 135 "Djenne, Living Tradition" *Aramco World* (Nov.- Dec. 1990) pp. 25-26

p. 136 Gibb, H.A.R., trans. *Ibn Battuta* (London, 1963) pp. 329-330
Decorative Frieze: Paccard, Andre *Traditional Islamic Craft in Moroccan Architecture 1* (France, 1980) p. 188

p. 137 Decorative Frieze: Refer to p. 136 above

p. 142 Quoted in: Zakaria, Rafiq *The Struggle Within Islam* (London, 1989) p. 286

p. 146 Decorative Frieze: Paccard, Andre *Traditional Islamic Craft in Moroccan Architecture 1* (France, 1980) p. 327

p. 149 Museum of Fine Arts, Boston

p. 152 Decorative Frieze: Refer to p. 136 above

p. 153 *Al-Hayat*

p. 154 "Muslims in the Caribbean" *Aramco World* (Nov.- Dec. 1987) p. 6

p. 156 "Calligraphy: The Art of Islam- in the Name of God" *Aramco World Magazine* (July- Aug. 1977) p. 26

p. 157 *Al-Hayat*

p. 158 "Muslims in Europe: the Mosques" *Aramco World Magazine* (Jan.- Feb. 1979) p. 10

p. 159 Decorative Frieze: Refer to p. 136 above

p. 160 "Ramadan in Holland" *Aramco World* (March- April 1990) p. 14

p.162 Decorative Frieze: Refer to p. 136 above

p.163 Decorative Frieze: Refer to p. 136 above

◆ STRAIGHT PATH

p. 173 *Al-Hayat*

p. 174 *Al Mostakbal* (January 28, 1989) Issue 623 p. 29

p. 175 Arabic/English Computer Keyboard: "Arabic and Arwri" *Aramco World Magazine* (July- Aug. 1983) p. 15
Arabic/English Labels: "From Suqs to Supermarkets" *Aramco World Magazine* (Jan.- Feb. 1981) p. 13

p. 176 "Ramadan in Holland" *Aramco World* (March- April 1990) p. 23

p. 179 *Al-Hawadeth* (January 27, 1989) N. 1682, p. 35

p. 181 Ahmed, R.S. *The Militant Prophet* (London, 1991) p. 212

p. 182 *Hassan Fathy* - A Mimar Book (London, 1985) p. 142

p. 184 "Calligraphy: The Art of Islam- In the Name of God" *Aramco World Magazine* (July- Aug. 1977) p. 22